T. M. KITWOOD

# What is Human?

INTER-VARSITY PRESS

INTER-VARSITY PRESS

*Inter-Varsity Fellowship*
*39 Bedford Square, London WC1B 3EY*

*Inter-Varsity Christian Fellowship*
*Box F, Downers Grove, Illinois 60515*

© INTER-VARSITY PRESS, LONDON

*First edition October 1970*

UK ISBN 0 85110 351 0
USA ISBN 0 87784 695 2

Printed in Great Britain by
Hunt Barnard Printing Ltd., Aylesbury, Bucks.

# CONTENTS

A QUESTION TO BE FACED     7

THE HUMANIST UNDERSTANDING OF MAN     10

    The forerunners
    The landslide of unbelief
    Putting humanity first
    Without supernatural aid
    Evolutionary ethics
    Doubts and dissatisfactions

THE EXISTENTIALIST UNDERSTANDING OF MAN     54

    Origins
    The tree of existentialism
    God is dead
    Life is meaningless
    Man becomes God
    The way of self-destruction

THE CHRISTIAN UNDERSTANDING OF MAN     92

    Existence with meaning
    The humanism of Christianity
    A moral failure
    The overcoming man
    Immersed in suffering
    The Christian way of knowing

TRUE TO OUR HUMANITY     130

SELECTED BIBLIOGRAPHY     133

INDEX     140

# A QUESTION TO BE FACED

Our generation is possibly the most enlightened that has ever been. We understand our environment to a remarkable degree, and our control of it goes forward with amazing speed. But are we also the blindest? We have not been successful in making ourselves happy, if we are to judge by the fact that fifteen people per day in Britain alone resort to suicide, or by the large and increasing number of mentally sick. Despite all our discoveries, do we yet understand what it is to be human?

Many new issues are being faced today as a result of advances in technology and medicine, and changed social conditions. In many countries the laws dealing with divorce, homosexuality and abortion are being or have been altered. Legislation about transplantation of organs of the body will soon be needed, and not long hence a test-tube baby may become a serious possibility. There is the problem of the elderly, now that they remain alive so much longer, with the allied question of whether it is ever right to hasten the death of an incurable sufferer. The population explosion becomes daily a more urgent issue and progressive urbanization, which could be man's greatest social opportunity, is frequently a curse. The next twenty years may well see half the world in a state of famine, while the rich countries will grow more prosperous than ever.

Any sound attempt to deal with these problems and a host of others can be made only in the light of some definite understanding of the meaning of our humanity.

Western society has accepted a great deal in the name of progress with amazing gullibility, because it has no clear human values. There are signs that the developing countries, too, in the urgent rush of self-advancement, are hurrying into exactly the same mistakes. My aim in this book is not to deal with detailed moral issues, but rather to explore the underlying question of what it is to be human, upon which all other answers must depend.

We must also try to understand what is human for the very simple reason that we have a human life to live. We must have some concept of a truly human existence in order to know what we are aiming at. No-one can reach maturity or a more than superficial happiness without at least having come to a tentative answer. Yet the great majority of educated men and women never ask this question seriously, and meekly join the crowd of those whose lives are impoverished because they have scarcely ever paused to think. For many people, the tempo of life when student days are over is such as to prevent this question being faced in tranquillity, until retirement or a long convalescence provide the opportunity. But 'What is human?' is the question that concerns us most of all.

The modern world has put forward various possible answers. Communism, for example, has a clear idea of what is human, even if history has condemned it as deficient. There seem, however, to be three main alternatives in the free West; secular humanism, existentialism, and Christianity. Each of these titles covers a variety of opinions, but nevertheless represents a distinct viewpoint. My aim is to bring the three together and compare them.

It might be objected that a convinced Christian is in no position to represent the other two views in a way that does them justice. I have certainly tried to give a fair account of humanism and existentialism, seeking not only to present the facts but to enter into their

8

spirit; with what success the reader may judge by referring to the original sources, some of which are listed in the Bibliography.

There is something to be said, however, for biased accounts, provided that the bias is openly declared. It is certainly more instructive than reading those who, claiming to have no bias, conceal their prejudice beneath a professed objectivity. For in the last resort there are no unbiased accounts. My aim is to present all three views reliably, but there can be no substitute for reading a humanist on humanism and an existentialist on existentialism. I can, however, justly offer a Christian critique of the other two points of view, and show both where a Christian accepts their insights, and where he feels they are deficient.

In the first two parts of this book I have tried to give an outline of humanism and existentialism, concluding each with a brief appraisal. Brevity has meant that drastic selection was necessary and that some historical statements have had to be made in such a sweeping way that their accuracy is very limited. Possibly my account of humanism is too much slanted towards biology, and my account of existentialism towards Nietzsche. But that is because my own studies have led me that way, and therefore I have more authority to write about them. The appraisal at the end of each of the first two sections has been only from the presuppositions that any critic might have, while the Christian evaluation is reserved for the third part and the final section.

If this book is offered to anyone in particular, it is to those many who have not found the way to a full Christian belief, either through misunderstanding or through ignorance of what Christianity really is, but who at the same time instinctively feel dissatisfied with what is offered in its place.

9

# THE HUMANIST UNDERSTANDING OF MAN

'What we have faith in is the capabilities and possibilities of man.'
Sir Julian Huxley.

'The faith of the humanist is first of all in reason, in the reliability of tested evidence.' H. J. Blackham.

## The forerunners

'Agnostic' – one who does not believe that for which there is no good evidence; 'secularist' – one who believes that the concerns of this present world are all-important; 'humanist' – one who puts humanity first; by these and other titles have the men styled themselves who seek for morality without God. Humanism thus makes its appeal as a way of uprightness without superstition, as something near to religion but without the intellectual tangles that belief in God seems to cause, as a philosophy of goodness for scientific man.

Yet though it appears at first to be a thoroughly modern movement, a product of the scientific age, it can justly claim an older tradition. The way of life which Confucius taught in ancient China, and some forms of Buddhism, were humanist in the sense that they placed the responsibility upon man to manage his life without reference to God. But humanists usually see the first real expression of their views in the Greek thought of the fifth century BC, when perhaps for the first time men began to make rational enquiry for its own sake. In other civilizations, such as those of Egypt and Babylon, the embryo disciplines of agriculture, building and mathematics were so tied up with superstition and magic that progress beyond a certain point became impossible. The Greeks, however, went far towards setting science and philosophy free. The objective use of reason is perhaps the greatest gift we have inherited from them, and it forms one of the fundamental principles of modern humanism.

The hard labour of Athenian society was done by slaves, which gave the aristocrats leisure to reflect and discuss. They learned what it was to theorize: to make rational speculations on the basis of empirical observation. In this atmosphere of free enquiry many steps forward were taken. Geometry became a strict intellectual discipline. Natural history was considered a subject worthy of study. Astronomy became a science in its own right apart from magic. The Greeks even conceived of a sun-centred universe 2,000 years before Copernicus. Medical practice was put on a sound basis by Hippocrates. In his precepts he wrote: 'In medicine one must pay attention not to plausible theorizing, but to experience and reason together. I agree that theorizing is to be approved provided it is based on facts and systematically makes its deductions from what is observed.' There could be no better statement of the method of experimental science.

The Greeks were the pioneers of democratic government, which meant that free political discussion could be indulged in with impunity. They produced some of the finest drama, sculpture and architecture that the world has ever seen. And they took religious thinking a long way beyond the common level of fear and superstition. By the fifth century most Athenians had rejected belief in the crude display of deities they had inherited from the Homeric past, which were much too fallible to be taken seriously. The affairs and intrigues of Olympus were no example for lovers of wisdom to follow. Some philosophers such as Plato were moving towards a high monotheism, while others were beginning to doubt whether God existed at all. At any rate, he was so remote from men that it made no difference.

In all this the humanism of today is foreshadowed: the rejection of tradition where it conflicts with truth; the need for discussion and careful unbiased enquiry; above all, the insistence on the use of reason as the only reliable means of knowing. The classic expression of the spirit and values of the Athenians is to be found in the oration at the funeral of Pericles, as recorded and imaginatively reconstructed by Thucydides, of which here is an extract.

'Just as our political life is free and open, so is our day-to-day life in our relations with each other. We do not get into a state with our next-door neighbour if he enjoys himself in his own way. . . . We are free and tolerant in our private lives; but in public affairs we keep to the law.

When our work is over, we are in a position to enjoy all kinds of recreation for our spirits . . . in our own homes we find a beauty and good taste which delight us every day, and drive away our cares.

Our love of what is beautiful does not lead to extravagance. Our love of the things of the mind does not make us soft. . . . As for poverty, no-one need be ashamed to admit it: the real shame is not taking practical measures to escape from it.

We make friends by doing good to others, not by receiving good from them. This makes our friendships more reliable. . . . Each single one of our citizens in all the manifold aspects of life, is able to show himself the rightful lord and owner of his own person, and to do this, moreover, with exceptional grace and exceptional versatility.'[1]

There are at least four great principles here. First, tolerance. We allow other people to enjoy themselves in their own way, respecting their individuality and not criticizing them for being different from ourselves. The law protects our community living, but does not interfere with private life, in which we may hold our own convictions and do what we please provided it does not harm our neighbour.

Then there is the ideal of wholeness or balance. A variety of occupations must fill the life of man, both work and recreation being needed for full satisfaction. The balanced man, too, makes use of all his faculties; his mind through thought and discussion; the artistic side of his nature through beautiful buildings, sculpture and the theatre; the body through athletics. The Greeks believed in personal fulfilment.

Third, there is the ideal of co-operation and generosity. We do good not for reward but for its own sake, with neither prohibition nor the hope of remuneration from religion. It is not necessary for good behaviour to be commanded; the need for it is self-evident to any educated man.

And there is the ideal of self-reliance. Every man should learn to master himself through discipline. He must use his own initiative to find a practical solution to his own problems, and though in relation to his fellows he is both receiver and giver, he is truly independent. He manages his own life through his own resources. There is no reference to God or the gods, as if for practical purposes they do not exist.

This, according to the Periclean vision, is the way of life that is true to man's inner nature. Living thus, he

[1] Thucydides ii. 37–41 (Penguin Books).

13

lives according to the laws of his own being. The ideals of tolerance, fulfilment, co-operation and self-reliance are all found in the humanism of today.

Perhaps the great mistake of the Greek scientists and philosophers was to rely too much on concept, too little upon observation. It was possible to erect a whole structure of ideas upon poor experimental evidence. Aristotle, the towering figure in Greek science, was one of the greatest biologists the world has ever known; but it was his physics and astronomy, which were less securely founded upon experiment, that so greatly influenced his successors. Aristotle's physical system was based on certain ultimate and universal principles which were intuitively perceived as correct, of which the most infamous was that all heavenly bodies must move in circles because the circle is the perfect motion. For 1,000 years this and other axioms of his were accepted as authority without being subjected to experimental test, a fact which contributed largely to the petrification of ancient physics.

Greek science reached its zenith during the third and second centuries BC in Alexandria, which under the Ptolemies succeeded Athens as the world's intellectual centre. But the emphasis in Alexandrian learning was increasingly on metaphysics rather than physics; speculation rather than empiricism became the fashion. Later it was here that Christian thought and Greek philosophy came into sharp confrontation, and some of the early Christian apologists such as Clement and Origen wrote to defend their faith.

In the seventh century, the Moslem invaders overran North Africa and Asia Minor and even pressed as far west as Spain. The learning of the ancients remained largely with them until, via Islamic philosophy, Aristotle was rediscovered by the Schoolmen. The Moslems added little to the ancient learning, nor did they extensively practise its humanism, but they did

14

bring it intact through the Dark Ages to the light of the Renaissance.

For about 1,000 years, from AD 300–1300, the dominant intellectual interest in Europe was theology. All the great scholars outside Islam, such as Augustine, Anselm, Aquinas and Bernard, were Christian divines. Their thinking even on secular affairs and natural history could not be dissociated from theology, for to them the whole of life could only rightly be seen in the light of eternity. Human values were almost totally considered to be Christian values. But during the Renaissance a non-religious humanism again emerged.

Largely through the rediscovery of the writings of the Greeks and Romans, and as the number of educated people increased, men began to ask some of the same questions as the Greeks had asked almost 2,000 years before. Once again men asserted their reason against superstition, and once again became intensely curious about the universe around them. It was during the Renaissance that modern science began.

In art and sculpture the portrait was developed. From Giotto onwards there was a gradual breaking away from the mediaeval tradition, and a new interest in men as men. Although for another three centuries the majority of paintings were religious in their subject, the real concern was increasingly with humanity. The greatest work of art of the Renaissance, the vast roof painting in the Sistine Chapel by Michelangelo, is probably a monument more to the glory of man than of God.

In drama, only a century lay between the morality plays, whose portrayal of character is flat and amateurish, and the greatest works of Shakespeare. He and those who wrote during the two succeeding centuries had evidently observed human beings closely. Frequently even in a minor part a distinct human being can be seen, the impression being conveyed perhaps by

15

one or two remarks. There is no overt intent to teach a religious or moral lesson. The aim, rather, is to portray the human situation and let it convey its own message.

The Renaissance, too, was a time of adventure and discovery. The crossing of the Atlantic by Columbus, the rounding of the Cape of Good Hope by Diaz, and the circumnavigation of the globe by Magellan were exploits that probably needed more courage in their day than a visit to the moon in 1969. The exploration of the world led rapidly to the establishment of foreign empires and a general extension of the European vision. It seemed that the spirit of man had been set free. Man was becoming self-reliant. He could achieve great things, and frequently without reference to God.

The word 'humanist' was itself coined at the time of the Renaissance. Its meaning then was a little different from today, because many of the Renaissance humanists were devout Christians. But the concern with humanity, the determination to explore the two worlds of environment and intellect, has much in common both with the Greeks and with the modern secular movement. The master-mind of the whole period, Leonardo da Vinci, epitomizes the humanism of the Renaissance. His knowledge of anatomy, meticulously compiled from experiment, would equal that of many modern doctors. His inventive dreams included helicopters, parachutes and breech-loading guns. He was an engineer and canal-builder. He even made a study of fossils. All this was achieved as well as his artistic output. Leonardo is one of the greatest of all examples of the many-sided man.

The humanism of the Renaissance had another and possibly more important aspect: the confrontation between reason and authority in matters of science and religion. In astronomy and physics great advances were being made. For more than a millennium astronomers had worked with the elaborate system of Ptolemy which, following Aristotle, described all motions of heavenly

16

bodies in terms of circles, with the earth at the centre. The doctrine of Aristotle that celestial motion was circular and that the heavens were beyond the realm of imperfection was almost universally held. Copernicus, however, after years of brooding and calculation, showed that it might be simpler to make the sun the centre. Later Kepler found himself convinced by the evidence, against his will, that the planets moved in elliptical orbits.

Traditional theology had become almost inextricably intertwined with Aristotelian philosophy and the earth-centred universe. Besides, the earth must be the centre, ran the argument, because it was the scene of Christ's coming. The sun must move because, according to the psalmist, 'he rejoices to run his course'. A clash was inevitable because the Roman Church, once committed to dogma, could not recant except by extremes of sophistry. The story is told that once a certain Father Scheiner mentioned to his superior that he had seen spots on the sun, to which he received the following reply: 'You are mistaken, my son. I have studied Aristotle and he nowhere mentions spots. Try changing your spectacles.'[2] So great was the authority of tradition, that it could decide in advance what men might see.

Galileo, the greatest and most tactless of the Renaissance astronomers, was the focus of the controversy between the church and the scientists. In 1609 with his newly-designed telescope he soon began to make discoveries about the heavens that were quite incompatible with Aristotle. He found that the Milky Way was an immense cluster of stars; that the moon, far from being made of crystal, appeared to have innumerable mountains and craters. He observed the satellites of Jupiter and, worst of all, saw irrefutably that the sun had spots.

Though advised by his friends to steer clear of

[2] A. E. E. McKenzie, *The Major Achievements of Science* (Cambridge University Press).

theological controversy, Galileo was irrepressible. He was admonished by the papal authorities neither to hold nor teach the theory of Copernicus. He ceased to teach it, but he still held it. Later, when a new pope had come into office, Galileo published his *Dialogue Concerning the Two Chief World Systems – Ptolemaic and Copernican*, a dialogue in the manner of Plato, which enabled the author not explicitly to state his commitment. But the commitment was so clearly implied that a few months after its publication the book was suspended, and Galileo was summoned before the Inquisition, where he was forced into submission.

Superficially the church was the victor. But by this time an overwhelming majority of intellectuals had decided for Copernicus. The long-term effect of Galileo's suppression was to discredit the authority of the Roman Catholic Church, which by many came increasingly to be seen as the great enemy of truth and progress. The church, resting blindly on the teachings of Aristotle and Aquinas, had been shown to be fallible. It was natural that its authority should be rejected.

But the church was also shown to be fallible in matters of religion. When Erasmus translated the New Testament from the original Greek he found that in a number of places the hitherto accepted version of the Bible in Latin had plainly misrepresented the meaning of the original writers. Then as men studied the Bible more closely, it became plain that the church was not teaching the biblical faith. Abuses which discerning thinkers had perceived long before were openly criticized and condemned. In the political and religious turmoil large sections of the Christian church broke away and sought to reform themselves. The authority of the church was again called in question, and against it was asserted the authority of the Scriptures and of human reason. It was from both these two grounds that the Reformers felt able to take issue with the church and tradition, so coming to a Christianity closer to that of the New Testament and more satisfying to their minds.

Scepticism about the church could very easily lead to scepticism about religion altogether, especially in countries where the church appeared to have closed its mind. At first the doubts had to be kept under a thin veneer of orthodoxy, though later it became acceptable to make an open show of unbelief. A process of questioning and doubting had begun whose more radical forms were the direct progenitors of modern humanism. The spirit of the times is clearly seen in the writings of Montaigne in the sixteenth century. Under a superficial conformity he frequently poked fun at the church; in the very best of taste of course, as was becoming to an educated Frenchman. In his longest essay, he gently mocks a theologian who 'undertakes by human and natural means to establish and verify all the articles of the Christian religion against atheists'. At one point he makes this perceptive comment: 'A persuasion of certainty is a manifest testimony of foolishness and extreme uncertainty.' This jibe against a church which claimed authority far beyond its legitimate field was much too pointed to be comfortable.

So between 1300 and 1600, in various ways the centre of man's interest changed. The church had pervaded the whole of life. Its authority, which had assumed such a gigantic place in the mediaeval scheme and had become manifestly absurd and overbearing, was broken. From this time forward many of those who believed took the Bible and their own conscience as surer guides. But there were others who went further, and looked to reason and science alone.

## The landslide of unbelief

We must now briefly pursue the history of scepticism through the centuries that followed the Renaissance, and see how the organized humanist movements came into existence.

After the great clash between reason and authority that occurred in the time of the Renaissance, it was inevitable that sooner or later doubt should be cast on all that was called knowledge and all ways of knowing. This was a destructive process, but on the debris were erected the new intellectual structures of rationalism, based as far as possible on reason alone.

The seventeenth-century philosopher John Locke questioned the sureness of our knowledge of the external world. He held that we can know only our experiences and sensations; we can never know things as they really are. All we can do is bring together our impressions and unify them to form some concept of reality. Half a century later David Hume pursued these ideas further. If all we can know is data from the senses, how can we distinguish between impressions that have their origin in the real world and those which are hallucinatory? To this question he could give no satisfactory answer. He even cast doubt on the most fundamental principle of the science of his day, causation; that is, the idea that one event actually makes another one occur. Hume's scepticism was so comprehensive that it rendered itself untenable; some of his answers were, to use his own words, 'cold, strain'd, and ridiculous'. Locke and Hume are only examples of the new doubting that emerged as a consequence of the Renaissance. There were others later to follow with a scepticism far more extreme.

A more optimistic view of science and reason also flourished in the eighteenth century, especially among the group of French intellectuals before the Revolution who came to be known as the *philosophes*, of whom the two most famous were Voltaire and Rousseau. The *Encyclopédie*, published over a number of years, contained their contributions on a wide variety of subjects. In print it was still necessary to maintain a semblance of orthodoxy, but much of what was written, damning with faint praise or ironical, was subversive of religion. A few of the *philosophes* were deists, believing in a distant Creator who had no practical dealings with mankind; others were atheists, though they could not be so explicitly; almost all were bitterly opposed to the church.

Positively, the *philosophes* were passionate believers in freedom of thought, in tolerance, in the use of the intellect. Man's chief objective, they held, should be the good life on earth, for which the first requirement is enlightenment, the liberation of men's minds from religion and superstition. Then, some of them believed, human nature could be almost indefinitely improved. Many of the *philosophes*, in theory at least, believed in democracy. The idea of liberty, fraternity, equality, which ran amok in the Revolution, sprang directly from their thinking. Some of their democratic convictions were embodied in the American Declaration of Independence, and much of their thought passed over into nineteenth-century England.

Jeremy Bentham, who has been called the first social scientist, applied some of the ideas of the Enlightenment to English political theory. His philosophy of utilitarianism was based on 'the greatest happiness of the greatest number'. All laws and institutions are to be judged by this. The principle is hard to follow out in detail because of the impossibility of computing happiness, but it gave an incentive to positive social action and the removal of oppression. Many of the great reforms of the nineteenth century had their origins, at least in part, in utilitarianism.

Bentham's intellectual successor, John Stuart Mill, was one of the most intelligent and broad-minded figures of the whole Victorian period. He wrote extensively on political subjects, perhaps his most famous work being the essay 'On Liberty', a careful analysis of the freedom of the individual in relation to the State. In some respects it is a precursor of the United Nations Declaration of Human Rights. By his writing and activity in Parliament (where plain speaking eventually led to his rejection), he greatly forwarded the principles of democracy and the values of truth, tolerance and compassion. Mill was a champion of the emancipation of women and one of the earliest advocates of birth control. Appropriately, he has been called the 'saint of rationalism', because of the way he lived out his own creed.

In France, contemporary with Mill, was the philosopher Auguste Comte. Having imbibed the French humanist tradition, he believed he had discovered the fundamental law of human progress. There are three stages in man's development. In the first, or theological, stage, human emotions are projected onto nature so that each natural phenomenon, like the thunder and the wind, is controlled by a deity. In the second, or metaphysical, stage, these deities are depersonalized and become abstract essences. In the third stage, all essences are discarded and the true, scientific relationships are described in empirical terms. This stage is called positivism. Comte's analysis of human thought deeply influenced humanism. Its implied view of history as progress has become, broadly speaking, the humanist view.

Comte's folly was to create, for the positivist stage, a new Religion of Humanity, complete with sacraments, saints and ritual. There were to be 2,000 churches in western Europe, and the supreme head was to be Comte himself. This extraordinary religion greatly affected the Victorians, embarrassed though they were by its more fantastic excesses. Mill and others actually sent Comte money when he was in financial difficulties. If Mill was a secularist cast in an austere and deeply Protestant mould, Comte was his colourful papist equivalent.

Unbelief was manifested in many different moods: the righteous wrath of a covenanter denouncing levity and superstition; the cautious questionings of a painstaking scholar; a wistfulness for the age of faith that had passed away. In contrast to all these, the most boisterous of the rationalists, Charles Bradlaugh, was a man of boundless energy and cheerfulness. In one year alone, he addressed 276 secularist meetings, four of which had an audience of over 5,000. In 1866 he founded the National Secular Society, the first organized movement of its kind. Bradlaugh loved to be shocking and sensational. One of his meetings was advertised as follows: 'The Bible: what it is: Being an examination thereof from Genesis to Revelation, intended to relieve the Society for Promoting Christian Knowledge from the labour of retranslating the Bible, by proving that it is not worth the trouble and expense.'[3] What William Booth of the Salvation Army was to popular Christianity, Bradlaugh was to the emergent secularism.

Perhaps it was the new discoveries of science, even more than the work of the philosophers, that gave impetus to what has been called the 'landslide of unbelief'. Gradually, as science advanced with explanations of more and more phenomena, it seemed that God was being edged out of the world. Already there were highly developed systems of astronomy, physics and chemistry, in which God had no explicit part. In the nineteenth century it appeared as if God were expelled from biology. This has often been attributed to Darwin, though that is an oversimplification.

Charles Darwin was not the originator of the idea of evolution; his own grandfather had openly propounded it. Darwin's great contribution was neither the idea of evolution, nor of natural selection, but a scientific theory of its mechanism. His central thesis was that, in the intense competition for nourishment and mates, only

[3] A. O. J. Cockshutt, *The Unbelievers* (Collins).

the fittest will survive and reproduce. Out of the prodigious birth-rate there will be occasional variants. Those which are better adapted to the environment will tend to survive, transmitting the variant characteristic to the offspring. Thus by an apparently haphazard process, millions of years of evolution have produced the variety of living species.

Darwin himself did not intend to remove God from biology, for when he began his work he believed in a Creator. But through his theory he appeared to have shown that the origin of all species, including man, was a result of blind chance and impersonal forces. Darwin himself in later life, to his wife's distress, lost his Unitarian faith. The *Origin of Species* is a long and tedious book, with examples painstakingly multiplied in chapter after chapter. Yet when the first edition was published in 1859 all 1,250 copies were sold on the first day, and about 30,000 copies were printed in the next twenty-five years. Clearly there were many who were eager to hear Darwin's message. At last there appeared to be a clear intellectual case for throwing off Christianity.

A year later the British Association met in Oxford for a debate on the theory, the leading speakers being Samuel Wilberforce, Bishop of Oxford, and Thomas Huxley who rapidly became Darwin's vigorous champion. Wilberforce, who was no biologist, spoke for half an hour against the theory in a verbose and scoffing manner. He even asked Huxley, in an ill-judged joke, whether he claimed descent from a monkey on the side of his grandfather or grandmother. Huxley's reply as recorded was: 'A man has no reason to be ashamed of having an ape for his grandfather. If there were an ancestor whom I should feel shame in recalling it would rather be a *man* . . . who plunges into scientific questions with which he has no real acquaintance, only to obscure them by an aimless rhetoric.'[4] His clear defence of

[4] A. O. J. Cockshutt, *The Unbelievers.*

Darwin's theory then and in the years that followed helped to bring its widespread acceptance. Once again a lack of integrity in the organized church was exposed.

Not only did evolution seem to demolish Christianity. It also appeared to provide a scientific basis for the philosophy of progress which was already widely held. If nature was marching forward to higher and higher forms of life, was not man doing the same? Not all evolutionists held this view, but some, notably Herbert Spencer, tried to build a system of thought upon it. The optimism of the secularists at the turn of the century was based at least in part upon the idea of evolution and, as we shall see, this view survives, though somewhat transmuted, to the present day.

Thus in the second half of the nineteenth century a new materialism arose. Science seemed to be nearing completion in its explanation of the world. Many scientists came openly into the offensive against religion and gradually claimed all territory, physics, chemistry, life, mind and spirit as their own. For those who discarded Christianity there was undoubtedly a gap which the new secularism appeared to fill.

During the nineteenth century there was a decline of belief among intellectuals in several branches of the church. The early efforts at biblical criticism in Germany led to great scepticism about the historical roots of Christianity. Very late dates were ascribed to many New Testament books, and there was a tendency to dismiss much of the Old Testament as folklore and superstition. The accounts of Jesus' miracles and resurrection were 'explained' by rational means. Jesus himself was gradually devalued into the Great Example, the Beloved Teacher, which he remained for many who would no longer call themselves Christians. The extreme sceptics even questioned the historical existence of Jesus. So the most liberal Christian view of Jesus gradually merged into that of the more reverent rationalist. Indeed in some 'lives of Jesus' it is impossible to label the writer Christian or humanist.

In England, where theologians were much more cautious about 'the accepted findings of biblical criticism', such radical views were not so widely held. By 1880, too, many theologians had come to accept that evolution might indeed be the scientific description, not of a blind mechanism, but of God's method in creating living forms. There was generally, however, a strong reaction against liberalism. On the one hand the Roman Catholic Church sought to strengthen its traditional orthodoxy, which was broadly opposed to evolution. The dogma of papal infallibility was promulgated in 1870. Many Catholics who were guilty of modernism were expelled from the church. On the other hand, some Protestant groups also had come to believe that evolution was heresy. In America there were even a number of laws passed to forbid the teaching of it in schools, the last of which was repealed only in 1968. Because the authoritarian attitude tended to lift the whole issue beyond the level of open enquiry, many with questioning minds were compelled into the opposite camp.

The Victorian period in England, for all its doubting, was one of intense moral fervour, so much so that the agnostics in their zeal for righteousness sometimes could appear more serious than the Christians. It was natural that many should seek for new, less dogmatic, modes of expression of religion. For those who no longer held the full Christian faith but did not wish to part with it completely, there was Unitarianism which maintained, as it still does, belief in God and a spiritual apprehension of life, without holding the deity of Jesus or the intervention of the supernatural.

Many new semi-religions appeared at this time. In America these included the first Church of Christ, Scientist and the Theosophical Society and in England the Society of Psychical Research. A number of new secular groups were formed in England following the pattern of the Society for Ethical Culture in New York, founded in 1876. These, besides attempting to carry the secularist message to the nation, aimed at fulfilling most of the social functions traditionally ascribed to the church; some of them even held secular services. George Bernard Shaw tells the story of a devout old Methodist woman who, on moving to London, inadvertently went to a rationalist temple, thinking it to be a Methodist chapel. She attended regularly to her dying day and, not noticing the difference, remained staunch in her Christian piety.

In 1896 the Ethical Union was founded, as a federation of the various secularist bodies, and three years later the Rationalist Press. During the following decades there was a general campaign to capture the minds of the expanding group of educated people, through cheap literature and public meetings, though its success was limited. The Ethical Union and Rationalist Press continued in existence, with much the same aim and basis, until in 1963 they were merged together in the forming of the British Humanist Association.

Broadly speaking, rationalism as an organized movement did not make great progress in England until after the second world war, when the international ties of humanism were strengthened, and nominal Christianity gradually ceased to be the fashion. Popular humanism reached its first nation-wide audience in 1955 when Mrs Margaret Knight gave two broadcast talks on 'Morality without Religion'. Since then humanist ideas have been ventilated with increasing frequency on radio and television. In America a group of secularists and liberal Christians published a 'Humanist Manifesto' in 1933, and an official Humanist Society was founded in 1949.

Finally, humanism has not lacked exponents among

the modern philosophers. The philosophical discipline has come increasingly to be the science of meaning and logic, an enquiry into what statements are meaningful and a search for criteria by which that may be judged. The majority of these thinkers, Bertrand Russell and A. J. Ayer, for example, have dismissed religious affirmations as meaningless and the religious quest as fatuous if well intentioned. These views have undoubtedly affected the general attitude to religion, and contributed to the rise of the contemporary humanism which we must now examine.

## Putting humanity first

There is now an international humanist network of considerable status, in which some twenty-five countries are represented, called the International Humanist and Ethical Union. The British Humanist Association is probably a fair representative, and it is at this body and its tenets that we shall look in detail.

The British Humanist Association has been in existence as an organized body for less than a decade, though, as we have seen, it continues the work of the nineteenth-century secular groups and claims to be part of a continuing tradition that goes back for more than 2,000 years. But these last few years have been crucial ones for the Association, first under the presidency of Sir Julian Huxley, and now under Professor A. J. Ayer, the well-known linguistic philosopher. During this time the leaders of the movement have sought to discard the less palatable parts of its heritage and to adapt it to the contemporary situation. Not many years ago the image of 'scientific humanism', as it was often called, was of a rather bedraggled, chip-on-shoulder company, anti-God and anti-church, provocative and tactless, and holding irresponsible views about sexual morality. Most of that has now gone.

Today the British Humanist Association puts out a very much more acceptable image. 'Humanists put Humanity first', to quote from one of their advertisements. They are concerned for human welfare, human freedom and peace. They now make their appeal less on filling the gap left by the decline of Christian belief, and much more on humanism as a positive way of life. Humanism stands on its own feet, whether Christianity stands or falls.

The British Humanist Association is a small movement, its roll of enlisted members being only a few thousand. It is nevertheless powerful, for it includes a number of leading figures in British intellectual, cultural and political life. There are about sixty names on the advisory council. Of these, some fifteen are professors, twelve are Fellows of the Royal Society and six are Members of Parliament. The British Humanist Association therefore is a concentrated organization. The humanists view themselves as a highly articulate pressure group, almost as a *corps élite*.

Where possible they will work within the movements that already exist – the Welfare State or UNESCO, for example. But if necessary they will create their own machinery. In politics the humanists have formed a parliamentary group of MPs and Lords which is not affiliated to any one political party; its aim is to promote humanist values, and to speak up for them in Parliament. A Humanist Broadcasting Council works to gain more coverage for their point of view on radio and television. There is a Humanist Health Council for those working in this field; and a Humanist Teachers' Association, to advise teachers and give particular help to those whose humanism brings professional difficulties. The humanists run courses for teachers of religious education. A counselling service operates to give advice and pastoral help to those in difficulty, but whose problem is not so acute as to need specialized assistance or psychiatry.

Thus the humanists are anxious for their voice to be heard in all areas of public life, because, they believe, they are representing the true interests of society and the convictions of a growing number of the population. They are also anxious to bring new people into the movement, through literature and through personal contact. They had a nation-wide recruitment drive in 1967, in the form of a 'Humanist Week' and another in 1969. There are now almost a hundred local humanist groups in Great Britain, and several regional councils. There is certainly humanism, and often an organized Humanist Society, in most British universities.

A general statement of policy was adopted by the Annual General Meeting of the British Humanist Association in July 1967. Its thirty-three articles cover such subjects as: international relations, war, disarmament; world population and resources; the shape of society; parliamentary and political reform, education; the arts, leisure and man's physical environment; the law and morality; censorship, religion in society; crime and penal policy, racial discrimination, civil liberties. The details of this document bear a striking resemblance to the United Nations Declaration of Human Rights, though the humanist statement is less pompous and better worded. It is also, naturally, geared to the specifically British situation.

The preamble to the policy statement is a general summary of the contemporary humanist view of life. It has evolved from earlier declarations, and in the manner of a religious creed is extremely carefully worded to avoid ambiguity or misconstruction. It must be quoted in full.

'Humanists believe that man's conduct should be

based on humanity, insight, and reason. He must face his problems with his own moral and intellectual resources, without looking for supernatural aid. Our concern is with this life, which we try to make worth while and sufficient in itself. We make no claims to special knowledge or final answers, since we regard the search for understanding as a continuing process.'

Two things especially emerge from this. The first is the humanist concern to make life worth while, and the second is the humanist self-reliance, coupled with rejection of religion in its traditional sense. These we must now examine more closely.

'Our concern is with this life' the policy statement declares. The humanists are well aware of the great problems that oppress the world, and are deeply concerned to find solutions. Some of these, such as world hunger, overpopulation, world health and education, are clearly to be solved by a simple pragmatic approach. The practising humanist is frequently drawn to work in these four areas of human need, and is to be found in developing nations, often working with great dedication and zeal. Because the humanists think strategically, they could never be satisfied with stop-gap answers. For example, they would not advocate trying to stave off world hunger by the rich countries giving food to the poorer. They could not accept a perpetual stream of doctors or educationists from the West going to the less developed territories, there to do works of charity. Therefore problems of this sort are only to be solved in the long term by the training of citizens of each nation to do the jobs in their own countries.

Christian work in such areas, based on missions, has tended to be patronizing, though Christians now are only too aware of the dangers of that attitude. But it is still possible to draw an unfavourable comparison between the mission hospital or mission school, largely run by expatriates, and the government-controlled organization which, though less efficient, is training its own citizens for leadership. It is to the latter that the humanist is naturally drawn, for he wishes to see men of all nations self-reliant.

Humanism thus finds itself completely behind the general campaign in developing countries to eliminate the three great social evils of poverty, disease and ignorance; and regards itself as doubly equipped to help in that struggle because it is free of moralistic or religious presuppositions, which can cause serious misunderstanding between men of different cultures. The British Humanist Association itself has played a part in the Bihar project, an international scheme to help rural development in India. It also gave special assistance to the first multi-racial co-educational school in Botswana.

The greatest world problem of all is international tension and warfare. In this area it is very much harder for the idealist of any kind to make a personal contribution. But the humanists may fairly claim to be as concerned about it as any. The United Nations Association itself is conceived upon broadly humanist lines.

In a less obvious way, too, humanism makes a contribution to world peace through science. One of the remarkable facts of the post-war years has been the way the scientists of nations of totally different ideologies have remained on speaking terms and shared their discoveries even while communication between their diplomats had broken down completely. The quiet fellowship of the scientists, many of whom are humanist in their ideals, and their inevitable interchange of ideas on subjects outside their field of work, may be in the long run a major factor towards world peace.

The humanists have a concern for the future of the world. The question of man's survival has now become urgent. Catastrophe could easily come to mankind, gradually through overpopulation, or suddenly through nuclear war. It is significant that at the conference on 'Survival' in Sweden in September 1969, attended by some of the greatest minds of the Western world, discussion was almost totally in secular terms and only one openly professing Christian was present.

Perhaps one of the most appealing things about the humanists of today is their determination to do good, and to do it in a thoroughly informed and scientific way. In one of their pamphlets on how to help the local community they claim: 'Humanists are not a bunch of cranks or a cold, dry, isolationist group who have opted out of the rough and tumble of living, but people who care in a practical and enlightened way for their neighbour.' The pamphlet goes on to give extremely sane advice on how to put this into practice, how to begin some project to help in old people's welfare or the citizen's advice bureau, or a club for deprived teenagers.

At present this sort of outreach is on a very small scale, but it has begun. The humanists in some towns have formed teams of visitors for hospitals and prisons. In Manchester they organized a private rehabilitation scheme for prisoners after their release. In Edinburgh they have established a centre for people without stable homes. They have three housing projects in London. They even have a society through which agnostics may adopt children. This has been necessary because most adoption societies insist on putting children into a home where the parents profess a religious faith.

This is the image of modern British humanism: a highly educated, alert, open-minded and far-sighted movement; optimistic, but soberly so, with a definite policy and programme for action; confident that it is a relevant way of life for today, and determined to communicate it.

### Without supernatural aid

This is the second item for detailed comment in the humanist creed. In this section we must look first at the humanists' attitude to established religion and then at their views on religion itself.

Humanism is a reform movement, aiming by all means to right certain wrongs in society which, it is felt, have been inherited largely from the so-called Christian past. Humanists in Britain regard as one of the most fundamental wrongs the assumption that theirs is a Christian country, and therefore to be subjected to Christian laws and Christian education. They point out that Britain is a very mixed community, with many religions represented (especially as a result of the immigration policy of the post-war years). Besides, the majority of British citizens practise no religious faith at all. Therefore any preferential treatment for Christianity, and any privileged position for it, is undesirable. Traditional laws which are based on a distinctively Christian ethic as opposed to general human values, such as those connected with homosexuality, abortion and divorce, should be repealed. By all means let Christians themselves pursue their own moral standards in the realm of sex or anything else, but let them not press them onto the community as a whole. By all means let Christians observe Sunday in their own way. But the humanists consider that to make society observe a Christian Sunday is just as unfair as to insist on total abstention from pork for the sake of a Moslem minority, or to forbid work on Saturdays for the sake of the Jews.

Further, the Church of England should cease to be officially involved, as it is at present, in the life of the State. Christian practices in law and Parliament, such as taking an oath on the Bible, should be abolished. If the monarchy continues, it should be secular and not publicly committed in its ceremonial, as for instance at a coronation, to the Church of England. There should be no preferential treatment in the mass media either for Christianity or for its Anglican form. The humanists call for the disestablishment of the Church of England. Let it take its rightful place, as the religion of a small percentage of the population.

One of the most strongly felt issues is the place of Christianity in education. Humanists protest strongly against the 'Christian indoctrination of the young'. They are unanimously opposed to the stipulation in the 1944 Education Act that there should be a daily compulsory Christian act of worship in all schools. They dislike the idea of denominational or sectarian schools, feeling that these do not give children a chance to make up their own minds. They would like to see religious instruction given in an unbiased way, so that children can learn about all kinds of religious and non-religious ways of life and come to their own decision.

Paradoxically, a number of Christians working in education hold similar convictions, for the different reason that they believe that a faith can never fairly be imparted when it is linked with school authority or taught by those who themselves are not committed. This has led in recent years to an alliance between Christians and humanists; they jointly published a report in 1965, and in 1969 they officially formed a 'Campaign for Moral Education'. The common ground between the two groups is a dissatisfaction with the present situation and a desire to abolish the compulsory religious assembly in schools. Both believe there is a distinction between 'moral education', which can be taught objectively in a classroom, and 'religious instruction', which can be done only by a committed believer and should never be compulsory.

It should be noted that humanists in Britain and elsewhere are not against moral education. They are as keen as any religious people that children should grow

35

up with moral values. They are anxious for children to know about the great religions, and would never wish to suppress information. But humanists insist that whatever religion or irreligion a child adopts, it should be his own, and freely chosen, not foisted on to him by his so-called education. When changes in the education laws in Britain do come, the campaign will exert strong pressure for a change in religious policy.

All that is to some extent a national issue, because the 'Establishment' in religion has survived for longer in Britain than in most countries. We must now deal with the wider question of the humanist view of religion itself.

All humanists are agreed that invocation of God or the supernatural is to be ruled out. But in their attitude to religion and in their views about a possible humanist 'church' they vary enormously. Some are against religion in all its forms. It is not difficult to find passages in the *Humanist Magazine* of the last few years that show great hostility, especially to Christianity. For example: 'What we should be fighting for is the total destruction of Christianity and its superstitions, impostures, and swindles.' Or this: 'I unhesitatingly declare that freedom from religion's myth is of prime importance to humanity.' Other humanists hold an almost mystical apprehension of life, and realize that spiritual problems are valid (even if traditionally presented in the wrong words), and put forward answers that have some touch of genuine religion. On this subject, it has been said, humanists can be divided into the crass and the sensitive.

In the old days of the Ethical Union and the National Secular Society, humanism at times looked very like an all-out anti-God campaign. Secularists from their soap-boxes could pile up as many proofs against God as the Roman Catholics would from theirs to show his un-doubted existence. George Bernard Shaw tells a story against himself about his early days of crass unbelief.

Once when he was at a party, the conversation turned to Moody and Sankey's current evangelistic mission. Shaw offered to repeat an experiment attributed to Charles Bradlaugh. He would challenge the Almighty, if he existed, to strike him dead within five minutes. This, he suggested, would settle the question of God's existence for ever. Despite Shaw's urging the company to put matters to the test of experiment, however, the embarrassed host managed to persuade him to desist.

This type of attitude to religion is frequently seen in undergraduate humanism, for example in the humanist group at one university which, at the time of a university Christian mission, circulated posters saying, in effect: 'Join the Christian Society now. Entrance fee: your critical faculty and your personal independence.' Bertrand Russell, as his group of essays published under the title *Why I am not a Christian* shows, was 'crass'. He was even capable of saying dogmatically that the three great emotions involved in the Christian religion are fear, conceit and hatred.

A much larger group of humanists, however, especially those who are older and have had to bring up children, and perhaps to suffer, are 'sensitive'. They realize that some of the deepest experiences of man are mysterious, and not fully accessible to reason. Humanists of this kind are often tolerant of Christianity when it is not superimposed by authority, and are certainly willing to work with Christians in the cause of human happiness, or relief of suffering, as witness a body like Oxfam. We have already seen how in Britain they are working together for reform in religious education. In December 1968, the Archbishop of Canterbury and other church leaders jointly with A. J. Ayer wrote a letter to *The Times* appealing for a cessation in the supply of arms to the Biafran war. This was the first united public action by the churches and the British Humanist Association.

Further than this, the humanists at times talk of some form of humanist religion, though exactly what this would consist of is not quite clear. Certainly it would not be a resurrection of Comte's Religion of Humanity nor would it have the Free Church style services of the old-time secularist chapels. It would probably include meditation, in the manner of Buddhism or the Christian mystics. It would be an attempt to resolve the inner problem of guilt feelings from which all suffer to a greater or lesser extent, aiming to achieve some sort of inner harmony, a unity of knowledge and purpose, which would lead on to more creative living. Julian Huxley, whose brother Aldous went a long way down the road of mysticism, is one of the most explicit on this subject. In a broadcast in 1960 he spoke of 'the possibility of enjoying experiences of transcendent rapture, physical or mystical, aesthetic or religious . . . of attaining inner harmony and peace which puts a man above the cares and worries of daily life'. It is clear that he sees life, in some sense, in religious terms. We will be looking further at his views in the next section.

Even the much less mystical H. J. Blackham recognizes that humanists have to make one or two assumptions which cannot be derived by reason and therefore are almost in the realm of religion. His two main assumptions are our responsibility for our own lives, and for the life of mankind. In this case the responsibility cannot be to God, or even to society. It is making oneself answerable to oneself. As soon as such a notion is admitted, humanism transcends utilitarianism completely. It also cannot strictly be called rationalism, for it has gone beyond reason. For anyone who holds such a view, another human being can never be a means, but is an end in himself. The need to respect and value other human beings is almost as compelling as if it were a divine command. The moral life is a way freely chosen because it is perceived to be worth while. This is a noble view to take, but any humanist who does so is in danger of opening the door fully to religious faith.

Thus there is a full gradation from outright atheism, through various forms of reverent humanism, to something very like religion. This in turn merges into extreme liberal Christianity. This century some theologians have tried to grapple honestly with the fact that there are unbelievers who hold human values almost identical to their own. Paul Tillich once said that any person who has some ultimate concern, some really serious commitment, some 'depth', cannot in the strictest sense be an atheist. Dietrich Bonhoeffer in his last imprisonment found himself thrown into the company of fellow-prisoners, some of whom, though not Christian, had compassion, humour and courage very like his own. Because he felt so at one with their ideals he sought in some way to include them in his understanding of the kingdom of God. It was this amongst other factors that led to his now famous remarks about 'religionless Christianity'.

In this sort of way some of the modern theologians have held out an olive branch to humanists, almost saying that they are Christians under another name. But humanists, even of the religious sort, are less willing to be embraced within a secularized Christianity. In general they prefer to remain outside. If, as happens from time to time, someone of broadly humanist convictions becomes a Christian, as in the case of Professor C. M. Joad or C. S. Lewis, they tend to come right inside, to a much more definitively Christian faith.


## Evolutionary ethics

Three possible bases for ethics have been put forward by humanists of the last 100 years. The first of these is a form of utilitarianism. This view suggests that happiness is the aim, and conduct should be directed towards achieving that for the greatest number of people. Because we live in society, certain conventions of behaviour have to be adopted or society would collapse. In this way a justification can be given, on pragmatic rather than idealistic grounds, for truthfulness, fairness, respect for property, and a certain sexual restraint. Such ethics are based on the general desire of men for happiness and some agreed idea of what makes a happy life. But beyond that the ethics may change as social conditions change. In no sense are they absolute, and they reduce most forms of moral behaviour to disguised self-interest.

A second approach to humanist morality we may term the ethic of assumed responsibility. This idea has been injected into the humanist bloodstream particularly by H. J. Blackham, who is clearly aware of the dangers of mere rationalism, and would reject the old term 'scientific humanism' as inadequate. He is anxious to create a 'full-blooded humanism' with values more profound. So, as we have seen, he suggests that a humanist must assume a responsibility for his own life and that of others, and go on to make a creative response to people and situations.

There is another basis for humanist ethics particularly favoured by those who have pursued some biological discipline. The early exponents of the view were Herbert Spencer and Leslie Stephen in the late nineteenth century; its chief modern advocate has been Julian Huxley, though a book like *The Naked Ape* by Desmond Morris shows an evolutionary approach to ethics on a much more superficial level. Such thinkers have sought for a basis for human conduct within the evolutionary process itself. For Spencer, the standard by which to measure good was the increase of length and breadth of life. That which achieves this is good; that which does not is bad. The process of evolution, Spencer believed, was directed towards that end. It is the modern version of this idea that we must examine in detail.

For the greater part of human history men have believed in some form of absolute ethic, binding on all men and in all conditions. The ancient Greeks held that the virtues were self-evident, like the axioms of geometry. The Christian church believes in an absolute ethic based on the moral law of the Old Testament and the teaching of Jesus. Even after the Renaissance, when the structure of mediaeval theology was crumbling, an absolute ethic was still widely held by unbelievers. Kant's theory of ethics still found a moral law binding on all men, based no longer on God but on the Categorical Imperative, the innate sense of 'ought' which seems to be part of human nature.

However, the eighteenth and nineteenth centuries saw a growing belief that ethics were relatively, not absolutely, based. Today there are almost no humanists who would claim otherwise. Several factors contributed to this change of view. One was the comparison of the customs of mankind in different parts of the world, a study which grew as world travel became more feasible. In one society it might be honourable to kill a man of the neighbouring tribe; in another, a widow might be buried alive at the funeral of her husband; in another, drunkenness was social conformity. Thus the growing science of anthropology showed that the *mores*, the customs, of different peoples could be almost radically different. This led to a questioning of the absolute validity of any moral code.

In more recent years the study of the mind has led to various theories about the origins of our moral sense. The Freudians, for example, tend to see it as a result of the early conflicts between dependence and aggression in the child's relationship with its mother. Some biologists claim to find the origins of morality in the behaviour of animals in the struggle for survival; for example, an animal's defence of a territory can look very like selfless action, and the formation of a pair-bond between male and female is seen as an adaptation for rearing of offspring with high intelligence, which need protection for a long period in early life. The details are not important here. But these sorts of reason have led those who have no religious beliefs generally to look for a new, more flexible basis for ethics. For many, evolution has appeared to provide an inspiring answer.

In 1893 Thomas Huxley, by then famous for many years, gave a lecture entitled 'Evolution and Ethics'. His grandson Julian Huxley gave a lecture in the same series in 1943, with the title 'Evolutionary Ethics', to commemorate the fiftieth anniversary. They came to surprisingly different conclusions.

Thomas Huxley's own life was firmly rooted in Victorian morality. He was perfectly prepared, intellectually, to admit that ethics had evolved. But he emphatically denied that any basis for ethics could be found within the evolutionary process. As he pointed out, immorality had also evolved. He distinguished between the 'cosmic process', which is evolution in the biological sense, under pressure from a nature 'red in tooth and claw', and the 'ethical process', which meant the evolution of man's moral ideas. The prevailing view of biological evolution was of a struggle for existence, the survival of the fittest, the destruction of the weak. All this, if applied to human society, would justify the crushing of the poor, the advance of ruthless capitalism, racial hatred, and many other inhumanities. Thus man's duty, in Thomas Huxley's view, is to curb the cosmic process, to prevent it from working in human affairs. Thomas Huxley believed in the evolution of ethics, but not in an ethic based on evolution.

However, the neo-Darwinists of this century have tended to see evolution in a different light. They have come to believe that co-operation just as much as conflict is a feature of the natural world. A living cell itself is a set of molecules whose functions are co-ordinated. At quite an early stage in the history of life, cells began to be connected both physically and in their function; the multicellular organism came into being. Later, in one environment several different creatures all co-exist, their biochemistry being complementary. One creature uses oxygen, another produces it. One excretes uric acid, another feeds on it, and so on. The higher forms of life have achieved quite advanced forms of social behaviour – community living, group hunting, a system of defence. The modern evolutionary philosophers see the possible precursors of human moral conduct in such activities.

Perhaps the Victorian evolutionists had made an emotive evaluation of the cosmic process when they felt that nature was ruthless and savage. The modern evolutionists, notably Julian Huxley and Teilhard de Chardin, have seen it as a grand march of progress, going on to the highest which we know, man himself. But they believe it does not end there because man's evolutionary possibilities are by no means exhausted. *The Phenomenon of Man*, Teilhard's famous book, cannot be read simply as a work of science. Rather, it is a prolonged poetic interpretation of evolution as the forward surge of life towards ever higher things.

Julian Huxley is confident in extending the term evolution beyond its Darwinian usage, meaning 'evolution by natural selection of the better adapted variant forms', to human society itself. Change occurs within society, as patterns of behaviour alter, as science, technology and medicine affect the life of man. Consider, for example, what revolutions of attitude have occurred in the last 100 years on the issues of birth control, or woman's role in society. This form of evolution Huxley terms 'psychosocial'. It is far more rapid than biological evolution, which took hundreds of millions of years. Now, a mere fifty years may see civilization change almost beyond recognition. Huxley believes that such a process holds enormous possibilities for man. There may well be a third stage in evolution, in which man both urges the process forwards and controls its direction. This he terms the 'purposive phase'.

From this interpretation of evolution, an ethic may be produced. As its basic axiom, the ethic holds that evolution is good. Therefore it must be allowed to proceed. Through experiments in living which may include selective breeding man must take the process forward. Such a view rules out of court any timeless or absolute moral principles, which are bound to change as social conditions change. But there is one absolute and unchanging factor – the process of change itself. Complete stability in society is undesirable, and any fixed pattern of belief is unethical. Both would put barriers in the way of progress.

So in his lecture Huxley offered three ethical principles, applicable to the three main areas of life: nature as a whole, human society, and the human individual.

> 'It is right to realise ever new possibilities in evolution, notably those which are valued for their own sake;
> 'It is right both to respect human individuality and to encourage its fullest development;
> 'It is right to construct a mechanism for further social evolution which shall satisfy these prior conditions as fully, efficiently, and as rapidly as possible.'[5]

These are of course only general principles, and need a great deal of working out and application to day-to-day situations. But their general tenor is plain. They are

[5] J. S. Huxley, *Evolutionary Ethics* (Pilot Press).

reaching forward to the new possibilities that the future may hold, to higher levels of co-operation between man and man, and to the enrichment of individual life through fuller development which brings new experiences. Morality is lifted as far as possible away from man in isolation, to man in relation to his fellows.

From these general principles Huxley found himself able to give some of the traditional values an ethical validity. Honesty and truthfulness have a high place, because these are essential for the free communication of ideas and co-operation between people. There can be no common knowledge, no body of science, without them. Justice is included, though not now based on the principle of retribution. Rather its basis is distributive – supplying to all men according to their needs. Faith is an evolutionary value, but it is now faith in man, and the high possibilities of his evolutionary future. Charity certainly is an evolutionary value too, but it must always be directed towards achieving those social changes which give men more equal opportunities, never the rich man giving to the poor in such a way as would stabilize the status quo. The evolutionary ethic tries to show the wrongness of oppression, because this benefits one part of society or one nation more than the rest. The evolutionary ethic demands fairness for all.

All works of science, all searches for new truth are specially valued, because these are the very means of progress. Works of art and music are seen as morally good, because they are the way to fuller development and awareness both for the artist and his audience. Even some forms of religious experience are considered valid. Not of course, the religion of personal salvation; rather, to use Huxley's own words, a 'discipline of the soul', a 'trained reverence', something akin to the mystic's heightened apprehension of life, and achieved through similar techniques, except that there is no theological content.

Finally, the evolutionary ethic covers the whole world. As evolution seems to aim towards greater co-operation on all levels, it is morally right to look for world peace, world sharing of culture, the pooling of scientific discoveries, and even for world government. All moves towards peace and unity between nations are to be encouraged, not only for the sake of the individual nation, but for the sake of the world.

Such is the evolutionary ethic as put forward by Huxley and others. Though it seems a little dated now, it has much more appeal than utilitarianism, because it offers man a vision of something much bigger than himself, and it seems less arbitrary than the ethic of assumed responsibility. It does, however, rest very much on a personal interpretation of evolution that goes far beyond science into a philosophy of optimism and progress. But what government by the proletariat is to the communist, and the coming of the kingdom of God is to the Christian, the forward surge of evolution to a better future is to many a humanist. It is the ultimate hope behind his creed.

## Doubts and dissatisfactions

Humanism appears to have much to commend it as a way of life for the twentieth century, suited both to countries that formerly were guided by a Christian church and Christian morality, and to those which are emerging from a primitive culture direct into the scientific age.

For here is a faith uncluttered by dogma and tradition. Humanists do not have to justify ancient beliefs to incredulous contemporaries. The humanist method, which aims at being scientific, is clean and precise. All assumptions are cut to the minimum. All findings are subject to verification, which is very appealing to the pragmatic spirit of our time. Scientists are simultaneously the most confident and the most humble of men: confident that their empirical method will yield a harvest of truth; humble about their own findings as no more than approximations to it. Humanism itself makes no greater boast because it does not claim to final answers or infallible truth. To the modern man, trained in scepticism, this humility and this confidence are very reassuring.

Humanism also brings a spirit of calm and order into a world where violence and chaos are escalating. The forces that lead to oppression and dictatorship are largely emotive and unreasoned; love of money, racial prejudice, blind ideological commitment. But the power of humanism is its appeal to reason, through which, if only its dictates were followed, the conflicts of the world might be eventually resolved. Humanism sets out to be a revolutionary movement, but the revolution sought is a peaceful one, through the co-operation of men of all nations who live above their passions.

The concern of humanism is very wide, far beyond the individual to the nation and the world. Even in ancient Athens the Greeks sought fair and democratic government. Throughout the Victorian period, the proto-humanists were insistent in their demand for social justice and recognition of the rights of man. Today many humanists have a vision for world government based on international democracy. For all their inadequacies, bodies like UNO and UNESCO are at least working towards that end. Humanism seems to be one of the very few non-totalitarian movements with an international concern for peace.

Humanism has a programme for the individual also. For it is a life-affirming creed, believing that this life is to be enjoyed thoroughly. It claims to offer a liberation from the chains of religion and fixed morality, and encourages each one to develop his faculties to the fullest

47

possible extent. It is a bracing creed with its challenge to self-dependence. According to humanism man must throw away his superstitious props – and live.

However, humanism has failed as yet to attract large numbers to its ranks and its practical outreach is minute. It shows little sign of ability either to become a really powerful movement or to give decisive moral leadership. I would like to suggest two weaknesses which may in part account for this.

First, humanism does not evoke a response from the whole person, intellect, will and emotion. It has an appeal for intellectuals, as witness the distinguished names on its advisory council, but it generally appears to be dull and uninspiring. It seems impossible to make it an attractive movement without cheapening its high ideals. A form of humanism is propagated through the popular press and the television, and even, it has been suggested, through the magazine *Playboy*. In these, non-religious values are often tacitly accepted and man is definitely self-reliant. But the image of the ideal man which they put forward is far too superficial to have the humanists' assent.

Humanists are at their best when involved in analysis and dissection, resolving a linguistic problem, making a social survey, assessing the value of some theory of ethics. But they lack originality when making positive statements about man's life, and easily descend to the platitudinous or gauche. Perhaps only a humanist could speak of a human being as 'a part of nature, a process continually renewed by its relationship to its environment with the conscious power to form meaningful concepts of the mode of activity of the world which sustains it';[6] or of love as 'a remarkable blend of a variety of responses to manifold drives, the profound effect of personal contact with a fellow creature being

[6] M. Laws-Smith, 'Faith and Materialism', *Humanist Magazine*, May 1969.

not the least of these responses'.[7] Using this sort of language, humanism cannot appeal to the ordinary man.

Discontent about this aspect of humanism is often expressed and publicized in humanist literature; the editors are scrupulously honest in letting the critical voice be heard. Not long ago there was a series of resignations from the Rationalist Press, apparently on grounds of its naïveté, insensitivity and emotional barrenness. The British Humanist Association document on sexual morals was widely criticized; to quote one humanist, it was 'self-satisfied and priggish'.

A very telling article appeared in the *Humanist Magazine* in 1964, entitled 'What's wrong with Humanism?' It was based on a serious letter written by one who had been a humanist for many years, deeply concerned to make the movement more popular, but who felt that it was too intellectual and almost 'clinically detached from life' to attract large numbers. The writer of the letter suggested that 'there should be a special Humanist Commission appointed to study the requirements of Humanism as a popular religious movement, with appeal to both intellectual and non-intellectual. A simple Humanist Bible and Humanist hymns should be developed. A ten commandments for humanists could be added, as could humanist confessional practices for groups or individual practice. Beliefs would, of course, be provisional, as it is a cardinal article of humanist faith that beliefs must change as new knowledge becomes known.

'The use of hypnotic techniques – music and other psychological devices – during humanist services would give the audience that deep spiritual experience and they would emerge refreshed and inspired with their humanist faith. . . .' Rarely is the dissatisfaction expressed with such openness and vulnerability. But it does

[7] H. Roshwald, *Humanism in Practice* (Rationalist Press).

seem that humanists themselves are chilled by the unspirituality of their creed.

A second weakness of humanism may be that it fails truly to reckon with the facts about human nature. Humanists are much more cautious now in making declarations about the improvability of man. The voice of evolutionary optimism heard a generation ago is now muted. But there still remains, to quote a leading humanist writing in 1969, 'a new hope of man's transformation of himself, the unquenchable Humanist faith'.[8] Without that faith humanism would die. But have humanists good ground for thinking that hope can be realized by the means that they propose?

It is undeniable that man's material lot has improved vastly through the coming of technology and medicine, and that many social wrongs have been removed through the application of justice and tolerance, principles fundamental to humanism. But is modern man with house, warmth, motor car, television, national health and social security any different in nature from his predecessors who lived a hardier life, or his brothers who still sleep on the earth and wear no clothes? John Stuart Mill wrote of his father that he 'felt as if all would be gained if the whole population were taught to read', so complete was his faith in the innate decency of man. Modern humanism, though not so naïve, still comes near to the same error. Even Bertrand Russell, well aware of the dangers of making unfounded or meaningless statements, once wrote: 'If we could learn to love our neighbour the world would quickly become a paradise for us all.' If, but how? It is at this point that humanism seems to have no solution.

Voltaire in *Candide* wrote a biting satire against the extreme optimists of the eighteenth century, which is still a cautionary tale for humanism. Candide, brought up in the optimistic faith of Dr Pangloss, faces a series of

[8] H. J. Blackham, in *Humanist News*.

shattering experiences which give the lie to the philosophy he has learned. At one point he asks a friend: 'Do you think that men have always massacred each other, as they do today, that they have always been false, cozening, faithless, ungrateful, thieving, weak, inconstant, mean-spirited, envious, greedy, drunken, miserly, ambitious, bloody, slanderous, debauched, fanatic, hypocritical, and stupid?' The friend asks Candide whether he thinks that hawks have always eaten pigeons. Candide agrees that they have. 'Well,' is the reply, 'if hawks have always had the same character, why should you suppose that men have changed theirs?' Modern humanism does not seem to reckon fully with this fact.

If this charge of naïveté is correct, perhaps it is the consequence of humanism being an aristocratic body, and as such insulated from some of the more terrible aspects of life. The Greeks had their slaves; the philosophers of the Enlightenment were largely from the privileged classes; the humanists of today come from the new aristocracy of intellect or merit. This is a strength for the movement, because it is made up of men and women of high quality. But it is a weakness too, for humanists are always in danger of underestimating man's folly and selfishness. Humanism may have been born in too comfortable a life-situation to be realistic for all kinds of men.

Humanism now faces a dilemma. While it holds a definite doctrine of man's moral progress and power to change himself, it certainly has a vision and an incentive. But this involves a belief about man which is increasingly hard to substantiate, and therefore is inconsistent with rationalism. But if such a belief is discarded, as some humanists would wish, not much remains. Humanism becomes more realistic, but is reduced to little more than 'do what you can'. Its positive assertions then become so diminutive that they

51

are almost worthless, and its power as a popular movement is even more curtailed.

The early humanists were sometimes suspected of irresponsibility, of using their creed as an excuse for evading the demands of religion or as a means of justifying sexual laxity. Today they have dispelled such suspicions. The striking thing, rather, is the quality which many humanists show in the way they live, a quality that cannot be justified on grounds of reason alone. Perhaps the best humanists already hold certain values, and later try to find reasons for them in evolution or elsewhere. It almost seems that they, too, like men whose religion includes the name of God, are believers when it comes to forming a moral code. The drab world of rationalism that they have created cannot ultimately contain the rationalists themselves.

If not from naked reason or from evolution, from where does the humanist ethic come? Its origin may after all turn out to be in the Victorian version of Christianity, handed on largely by those families and institutions that have preserved Christian values for several generations beyond the waning of belief. Not many humanists would admit this, and it would not be in place to pursue the argument here, because a Christian judgment is involved. It is, however, an empirical question open to verification as time goes on, whether humanists are accruing moral capital or living on the reserves of the past.

So for all its many qualities humanism is still deficient. To quote from an article by Geoffrey Moorhouse: 'The humanists are on the side of the good and the righteous and even the Christians know it now. If there is anything regrettable about humanism it is its absolute respectability . . . the humanists have become more sober than a chapel full of deacons. They engage in no internal controversies worthy of the name. They are not known to make public asses of themselves. They seem,

52

somehow, sometimes to be lacking something – some splendidly comic strain – of humanity.'[9] Perhaps this is why, though many are in sympathy with their ideals, there are so few committed humanists. Not many have judged it a sufficiently human way of life.

[9] An article in *The Guardian* of a few years ago.

# THE EXISTENTIALIST UNDERSTANDING OF MAN

'And only now does there come to man the great terror, the great prospect, the great sickness, the great disgust, the great seasickness.' Friedrich Nietzche.

'Total responsibility in total solitude – is not this the very definition of liberty?' Jean-Paul Sartre.

## Origins

During the last fifty years, and especially since the war, a stream of plays and novels which would have amazed and scandalized the Victorian moralists has appeared in Europe and America. Violence and perversion have been portrayed without any implied condemnation. All restraint in the treatment of sex has been abandoned. The London stage has seen dismembered characters conversing from garbage-cans, Queen Victoria as a lesbian, and the stoning to death of a baby, to give a few examples from recent years. Within the pop-culture there have been such productions as *Hair*, the exuberant, free-love, live-for-the-moment musical, or *Tommy*, an opera about a blind, deaf and dumb boy who grows up into a world that hates and sexually abuses him, until he gets his revenge in the same way. Perhaps the ultimate in this trend is the play *Breath* by Samuel Beckett, recent Nobel prizewinner: duration thirty seconds, no actors, no dialogue, and its props miscellaneous rubbish. The thing which would have shocked the Victorians more than anything else is not the apparent immorality of some of these productions, for that was well known in their day, but the underlying implication that there is no meaning or moral code at all.

It would be easy to dismiss all this as mere sensationalism. Some of it probably is. But the spirit of an age is reflected in its literature. It is clear that the recurrent themes of man's frustration and bewilderment, his alienation from his fellows, his attempts to right his wrongs through love or simply sex, his disillusionment and even suicide, are very much related to the contemporary world. This is the age of futile wars, of potential annihilation through a nuclear bomb, the age of protest and of moral anarchy. The post-war generation, especially, has seen the crumbling away of almost all those structures in which the Victorians placed their hope.

In the middle of the nineteenth century, the period when modern humanism was born, the general intellectual mood in Europe was one of self-congratulation. Through enlightenment it seemed that peace, virtue and humanity were steadily replacing the barbarism of former ages. Science was bringing more and more insight into the natural world, and greater control of the environment. Even the established church, despite rumblings from Germany where the biblical critics were at work, and the setback of the first clash with Darwinism, was generally smug in its orthodoxy whether Protestant or Catholic.

These two illusions of security, the one in secular and the other in religious thought, were later to be shattered by the upheavals of the twentieth century; the first world war, the Russian revolution, the depression, another great war and all that has followed it. Besides this, there has been a transformation of almost all areas of knowledge, scientific, sociological, psychological and religious. But long before these events occurred they were foreseen by two very sensitive thinkers who were largely neglected or ignored by the intellectual world of their time. One, Søren Kierkegaard, was a devout if highly unorthodox Christian. The other, Friedrich Nietzsche, was a violent atheist. As pioneers of that way of thinking which we now call existentialism, they have proved in many respects to be the prophets of the modern mood.

They both found themselves in revolt against what they felt to be the shallowness and inadequacy of the philosophies of their day. First, they were reacting against an optimism which seemed to them to be quite unjustified. Owing to growing material prosperity, social reforms, and above all the great strides forward of science, it was a time of unparalleled confidence. Evolution had for many almost become a religion (and so, as we have seen, it still survives in the evolutionary ethic of Huxley and others). The belief was widely held that progress was an inevitable law of nature. Therefore man himself was progressing. The smug effusions of the Victorians now seem laughable for their naïveté, but in those countries with a strong bourgeoisie and an established morality, usually based on second-hand evangelical faith, it was genuinely believed that the world was getting better and better. The church, also part of the bourgeois phenomenon, was well settled into a comfortable and established routine.

Kierkegaard, however, felt that the church in Denmark was no longer standing for real Christianity. It had a message which was popular and safe, which hid from people their true state before God. The preachers failed to bring people to that sense of guilt, anguish and near-despair which Kierkegaard believed must precede a vital experience of Christ. 'They have healed the wound of my people lightly, saying "Peace, peace", when there is no peace.'

Nietzsche, reared in Protestant middle-class Prussia, also perceived that all was not well. He foresaw that despite appearances the world might be thrown into a chaos worse than it had ever known. He foretold violence and calamity, sensing that those destructive forces were already at work which led to the two world wars. Part of his mission was to expose the inadequacy of conventional thought, and to awaken men to the realities which lay behind the appearance of stability.

Secondly, both Kierkegaard and Nietzsche were reacting against reason. For the thinkers of the nineteenth century had an almost unbounded belief in reason as the highest faculty of man, through which the great steps of progress had been made, and through which the natural world would soon be fully understood. In 1892 it was even possible for Michelson, famous for his measuring of the velocity of light, to say that probably 'most of the grand underlying principles of Physical Science' had by then been established, and the remaining work of science would be largely application.

In fact the nineteenth-century rationalists, without being aware of it, had violated their own principles and made an act of faith – in reason. It is impossible to prove by reason that reason has an absolute validity, that this is the method *par excellence* by which men come to a true knowledge of the world and of themselves. The most that can be claimed is that it appears to give consistent results. But there were those who questioned the place given to reason. This was not just on intellectual grounds but, rather, was due to an intuitive feeling that reason alone could not do justice to the profounder experiences of man, his loves, hopes, fears, dread and anguish.

Kierkegaard as a Christian hated the way that reason and theological systematization seemed to have drained the faith of power and saving vitality. Nietzsche, as an atheist, dissociated himself from the scholars of his day. He likened them to mills which grind the living seed to a dead powder, rather than planting them and allowing them to grow; and to clocks which need to be wound up, dull and utterly predictable. He hated the dryness and detachment of the traders in logic, and the barrenness of their deliberations.

As science progressed the personal and subjective were eliminated as far as possible. Instruments, which are utterly unbiased and much more predictable, are preferred to human beings. For science is concerned with questions of quantity, how much, how long, how fast, which instruments can measure more efficiently. Questions of quality and judgments of value lie beyond its scope. It is clear, then, that science is not competent to deal with our subjective life. The deeper questions of our existence can be faced by us only as human beings, not as scientific observers.

Putting it another way, the scientific method requires from us as much detachment as possible, but on the questions which concern us most we are inevitably involved. Instruments may tell us whether it is possible to make a nuclear bomb, but they cannot tell us whether to explode it. The scientists may design ways of controlling conception, but they cannot as scientists decide how to use them. So existentialism seeks to re-establish the importance of the subjective. Kierkegaard wrote: 'Passion is the real thing . . . the age in which we live is wretched because it is without passion.' And of science he wrote: 'The whole of science is a parenthesis', meaning that it has no concern with the important, personal issues of life.

Karl Heim defined an existential statement in this way: 'A proposition or statement is said to be existential when I cannot apprehend it or assent to it from the standpoint of a mere spectator, but only as the ground of my total existence.' Thus 'My wife weighs nine stone', 'My country has a population of fifty-seven million' are factual, scientific statements. But 'I love my wife', or

58

'My country is so dear to me that I would die for it' – these are existential statements. This takes us some way beyond Kierkegaard and Nietzsche, but these ideas are implicit in what they wrote.

Perhaps, though, the most disastrous exposure of the inadequacy of reason has been through the discoveries of psychology. Long before the advent of psychology as a science, Pascal wrote words which may be translated: 'The heart has reasons of which reason knows nothing.' This is a fair summary of what has been found about the underlying causes of human conduct. We are motivated at a level deeper than reason. A mass of drives, instincts, fears within us has been discovered, which like an iceberg reveals only a fraction of its bulk above the surface. It is now beyond doubt that we are motivated by factors of which we are at best only partly aware. We may be relied upon to rationalize – to invent reasons for – our conduct while its origin lies deeper in the unconscious. Reason is thus seen to be an activity on the surface of the mind, a mere cerebration. Even the scientists, avowedly the most dispassionate of men, have often been known to cling on to their theories on emotive grounds in the face of evidence to the contrary. Much of the argument in cosmology today may appear a generation hence to have been dictated by vested interests.

Now both Kierkegaard and Nietzsche, perhaps from the depth of their own introspection, had profound insight into human motivation. Nietzsche even termed himself 'the psychologist'. Even by the time of his death in 1900, psychology and psychiatry were still infant studies, but the early existentialists had already intuitively understood the main fact that these sciences were later to expose.

Finally, the reaction of existentialism is seen as the philosophy of man-by-himself. The findings of science are available to all for verification. Though they may have been discovered by an individual, they then

59

belong to all. In that sense they are impersonal, for the scientist believes that any intelligent person with the correct apparatus would make the same observations as himself. Science is a body of common knowledge, a collection of things-which-are-known.

In the nineteenth century this idea was commonly held outside its legitimate field. Reason had almost come to mean 'the consensus of opinion of all right-thinking people', applied to the accepted social conventions and the accepted moral code. Nietzsche, who hated the idea of generally accepted values, frequently raved against the bourgeois mentality in which he had been reared. The 'grand underlying principles', to use Michelson's phrase, he despised as the props of those too afraid to live. 'The consensus of opinion of all right-thinking people' he deplored as the attitude which prevents each man from true self-expression.

This is why the novelists and playwrights have tried for fifty years to shock us out of convention. Those who follow the crowd make no great decisions for themselves; they take refuge in the accepted ideas. They do not assert their individuality. The existentialist, however, has no principles to follow, for he believes there are none. He mistrusts reason as his guide. For him there is no universal truth. There is only the 'truth-for-me'.

One of the early humanists, Sir Leslie Stephen, writing in 1873, put forward the view that all ethical systems say much the same thing, that all differences in doctrine are superficial: 'The one objectionable theory is to believe anything very strongly; that is bigoted, and makes a man painfully narrow-minded. Look at all religions from the serene height of philosophy, and you must admit that all are beautiful in their way and may be turned to account by the genuine liberal.' He was truly expressing the common belief of his day. But existential thinking is almost totally opposed to this. For the existentialist there are millions of ethical systems in the world, as many as there are men. The vital thing is to believe whole-heartedly, to be bigoted, if that word really means committed to strong views. One must descend from the serene but useless heights of philosophic detachment and work out a way of life that is truly one's own.[1]

## The tree of existentialism

So far we have seen how existentialism came about as a reaction, against optimism, against reason, and against all those forces which deprive man of his individuality and reduce him to something less than a person. This is, however, a simplification, because the existential way of thinking has been present to some extent in all ages. The French writer Emmanuel Mounier,[2] in tracing the origins, draws a tree which shows the roots of existentialism in ancient thought, then the main trunk and the various branches which have grown from it.

One of the roots is Socrates who, in contrast to the Greek scientists, believed that the one fit object for human investigation was how to lead the good life. For him the subjective concern was far more important than learning physics. Another root is the philosophy of Stoicism, which held that men must accept life courageously, making the best of it, with no religious hopes that death might not be the end of all things. Another root is Augustine, who insisted that faith must come before reason in all true knowledge.

The trunk of the tree contains Blaise Pascal, a Jansenist thinker in the seventeenth century who in many respects anticipated Kierkegaard in the nine-

[1] For a number of ideas in this section I am indebted to P. Roubiczek, *Existentialism, For and Against* (Cambridge University Press).

[2] E. Mounier (trans. Eric Blow), *Existentialist Philosophies, an Introduction* (Barrie and Rockliff).

teenth. We believe in God, he said, rather like accepting a wager. We make it without intellectual proof, and on it we must stake our all. 'Let us weigh the gain and loss. . . . If you win, you win all; if you lose, you lose nothing; wager, therefore, that he is, without hesitating.' It is clear that Pascal is rejecting the intellect as the final arbiter, and asking for commitment. In his writing, too, there are many indications of that dread in the face of life's momentous issues, which is so commonly found in the later existentialists.

The main part of the trunk of Mounier's tree is taken up by Kierkegaard, who is certainly the father of religious existentialism. From early years he had been both attracted and repelled by Christianity. On the one hand it seemed to make almost inhuman demands; intellectually it seemed to him absurd. Yet he was drawn to it, irresistibly, until he became a Christian. He had once written: 'The thing is to understand myself, to see what God wished me to do; the thing is to find the idea for which I can live and die.' Such a truth he termed existential. For him that proved to be the Christian faith; but if God were omitted from Kierkegaard's statement, it would sum up the thought of many of the atheists who followed in his steps.

Kierkegaard believed that to follow Christ means renunciation of the world, the breaking of all ties, the abandoning of all wordly hopes, especially those most cherished. Abraham was a key figure in his thinking. For Abraham was called upon to sacrifice his son in whom his love and highest hopes were placed. God, it seemed, required him to commit himself to an action that not only caused him intense anguish, but was fundamentally against reason. The Christian faith was like that for Kierkegaard, a continued act of violence to his human desires, a constant tension, a commitment to absurdity.

Kierkegaard was summoning men away from speculative theology, away from formalism, back to absolute commitment. In this sense he stood against reason, for although he did not dispense with it altogether, he realized that there was a point beyond which it cannot go. That is where the existential decision must be made. Kierkegaard's own life was in most respects a failure to achieve the ideals he so forcefully preached. But the fact that his work has been so widely read and acclaimed this century indicates that for all its excesses his protest finds an echo in many modern minds.

After Kierkegaard, the tree of existentialism branches out. On one side there is Nietzsche, who has a special bulge all to himself, from which come Heidegger and Sartre. This, the atheistic line of existentialism, is commonly and rightly held to be the main one. It is this that we are to look at in detail, chiefly through the philosophy of Nietzsche. But Mounier shows us that it would be quite incorrect to associate existentialism only with its atheistic exponents; it is a much bigger thing than that. Several of the other branches of the tree are religious. It is probably true to say that two-thirds of modern theology has been an attempt to reassess the Christian faith in the light of existentialism, or even to use existential categories in order to reinterpret the Christian faith. To what extent are the 'truths' of religion simply statements of personal experience? Is the Bible itself a record of experiences rather than a set of universal truths? Can the Christian faith in any sense be set out as a series of propositions? These are the sort of questions with which some of the modern theologians have grappled, coming to various conclusions.

A little more must be said about existentialism in relation to theology before we come to the atheism of Nietzsche and others. One branch of Mounier's tree is given to Karl Barth, who more than any other figure has overshadowed the theology of this century. He received his training in the fashionable liberal theology verging on humanism, that tended to reduce the religion of Jesus to 'the Fatherhood of God and the Brotherhood of man'. But in 1914 he discovered that almost all his theological teachers had added their signatures to a declaration supporting the war policy of the Kaiser, a fact which for Barth destroyed the validity of liberalism for ever.

Besides this, Barth found that the liberal message had little to say to those who were living in the fear and insecurity generated by the war. He came to see that the Christian message was much more drastic than an appeal to man to exert his natural goodness. The New Testament included both an outright condemnation of man in his efforts at morality, and the possibility of total renewal through God's grace. Barth believed that the truth about God could not be found by man's own efforts. God is not known through observation and reasoning, in the same way as we 'know' the facts of science. He makes himself known through Christ alone, his Word, and reveals himself in personal encounter.

The appearance in 1919 of Barth's commentary on Paul's Letter to the Romans, in which some of these thoughts were expressed, has been likened to the explosion of a bomb in the playground of the theologians. It came as a forthright summons to return to real Christianity, the religion of Paul, Augustine and Luther. After the war, when liberalism was a lost cause, it seemed that Barth's theology might have a message for a disillusioned generation. Though Barth was never an existentialist, his thinking, which was so much influenced by Kierkegaard, has a close affinity to existentialism in its wider sense.

One other branch of Mounier's tree which deserves mention here is the Jewish theologian Martin Buber. In 1923 his famous book *I and Thou* was published, in which he taught that there are really two kinds of relationship, which he termed 'I-thou' and 'I-it'. 'I-it' is the relationship of observer to observed, of user to object. It is the impersonal and scientific, though it can exist and often does between persons. It gives us little understanding of ourselves. But the other kind of relation, 'I-thou', is the personal, the subjective. To undertake this an individual must go out of himself to meet other persons. Thus Buber could even say, 'All real life is meeting.' It is in the encounter with the other that we discover what life really is, we discover ourselves, and we meet the one who is addressing us in every human encounter, God himself. This too is a form of existentialism in its repudiation of objectivity and detachment, and its insistence on the personal.

The tree of existentialism has thus borne many different kinds of fruit, everything from the warm humanity of Buber to the pessimism and savagery of some modern plays. But we must now return to that branch of existentialism that is normally associated with the name, the atheistic movement of Nietzsche, Heidegger, Sartre, and others; particularly to Nietzsche, who was perhaps the most original thinker of the three.

Friedrich Nietzsche was born in 1844. His father, who died before he was five, and his grandfather, were Lutheran clergymen. He was intended also for the ministry, but at university he soon began to think otherwise, through his reading of the Greeks and the sceptics. At twenty-four his intellectual gifts were already widely recognized, as shown by the fact that although he had not yet obtained his doctor's degree, he was elected to the chair of philology at Basle. There he became a Swiss subject. In 1871 he volunteered as a medical orderly in the Franco-Prussian war, and after a brief spell of service returned with his health – mental maybe as well as physical – broken.

In 1879 Nietzsche resigned his chair on grounds of ill health, and obtained a pension. He lived in Switzerland and Italy, usually in boarding-houses, where he produced his finest work. An eyewitness has recorded his way of life at this time: his fastidiousness about his food; his insomnia which he sought to conquer with a formidable array of drugs; his cold, barely-furnished room in which, wrapped up in overcoat and scarf, he wrote for hours on end with his short-sighted eyes close to the page. Yet this withdrawn little man was transformed when he turned to writing. On paper he was capable of the most exquisite tenderness, the most brilliant sarcasm, the most passionate invective. He is the most readable of all philosophers, because the most poetic.

The tragedy and paradox of Nietzsche is epitomized in the last notable event of his life. The man who had written: 'Woe to all lovers who cannot surmount pity'; who had given his followers a new law, 'Become hard'; saw a coachman in Turin flogging a horse, threw his arms around it, called it his brother, and burst into tears. A few days later he broke down, insane, and remained so for some ten years till his death in 1900, by which time he was already world-famous.

It might be objected at the outset that a man who despite his intellectual brilliance was so obviously inadequate to face life is disqualified from giving others advice about their personal philosophy. This may have an element of truth. But is it not also true that sometimes the near-mad are endowed with special insight? So much of what Nietzsche foresaw has been fulfilled that he has been clearly vindicated as a prophet of our time.

## God is dead

Nietzsche's most enduring work is *Thus Spoke Zarathustra*, in which he declares his vision of the predicament and possibilities of man. It is cast as an epic poem, didactic in tone, luxuriant and highly evocative in style. The hero is Zarathustra, the all-wise teacher who shares his wisdom with his disciples and with all mankind. Nietzsche chose Zarathustra as the teacher's name because, historically, in his view, the Persian prophet Zarathustra (Zoroaster) was the first to propound morality, which Nietzsche believed to be man's greatest error. Therefore in this book he must now revoke his past and become the prophet of amorality.

The opening scene shows Zarathustra in his mountain retreat, about to go down to share his wisdom with mankind. As he descends he has a highly significant encounter with an old hermit who has devoted his life to God and spends his days in worship and meditation. Zarathustra talks a little with him, and when he has left him murmurs this to himself: 'Could it be possible! This old saint has not yet heard in his forest that *God is dead*!' Thus, suddenly, dramatically, the first and central theme of the book is introduced. God is no more. What consequences does that have for mankind?

Zarathustra goes on to a town, where he begins to give his teaching to the people. While he begins his teaching, as if by coincidence events occur which illustrate what he has just been saying. In the market-place of the town there are two towers and a rope is suspended between them, high above the crowd which, we are made to feel, is gazing up in expectation. A tightrope walker comes out of one tower and begins to cross on the rope. When he is half-way across, a brightly-dressed character like a buffoon appears. He catches up with the tightrope walker and springs upon him, demanding that he should make way for him. As the crowd falls apart in confusion, the tightrope walker crashes down.

Zarathustra comes up to the dying man to comfort him, assuring him that he need not fear death. There is, he says, no God to judge and no hell in which he might be punished. In the evening, when the crowd has departed, Zarathustra takes the corpse away for burial.

This is a parable of the human situation, whose detailed interpretation will become apparent later, but a clue is given in Zarathustra's own words: 'Man is a rope, fastened between animal and superman . . . a dangerous going across, a dangerous wayfaring, a dangerous looking back, a dangerous staying still.' It is a parable about a man who failed to reach the goal, and of another who displaced him.

The central part of *Thus Spoke Zarathustra* contains the teacher's discourses on a variety of subjects. In the last section Zarathustra is again in his mountain fastnesses, his task of instructing mankind complete.

Such a fantasy may seem an unlikely way to teach philosophy. The book is uneven in quality because it is too long to sustain its brilliance, but it contains a wealth of ideas from which later writers have borrowed, including almost all the main themes of atheistic existentialism. *Thus Spoke Zarathustra* has been picturesquely likened to a collection of sapphires embedded in mud.

'God is dead' is the statement which underlies Nietzsche's whole diagnosis of man. The one who falls off the tightrope is the believer, who has reached as far as he can in the progress of humanity towards a higher state. But now an unbeliever displaces him. This is Nietzsche's way of saying that the age of religion is finished, and the usefulness of religion is exhausted in helping man in his advance from animality.

Nietzsche is probably the most vehement atheist ever to commit himself to writing, yet he almost always prefers the statement 'God is dead' or 'God has died' to the straightforward atheist pronouncement 'God does not exist'. This is entirely consistent with the existentialist view of knowing, in which experience is considered of more validity than detached objective statements. So 'God is dead' is not so much a statement of fact as of experience. Nietzsche believed that mankind no longer felt God as in the so-called Age of Faith. The Christian religion, he believed, had in truth lost its hold, though the momentum of the past was still continuing and an apparently flourishing church was still in existence. Perhaps in some way, realizing that so much of what went in the name of piety was mere formalism and already dead, he foresaw that widespread departure from religious observance that has only become a reality in the last twenty-five years.

This loss of faith, Nietzsche held, was a fact of overwhelming significance, vastly more ominous for mankind than the events historians normally consider to be important. Our whole civilization, our laws, our values, are based on Christianity. But if Christianity is no more, then the undergirding of our society is broken, and the civilization and its values will disappear. Nietzsche did not hold, as did the majority of nineteenth-century rationalists, that Christian values could remain without the Christian God because they had a validity all of their own, independent of religion. He could thus foresee the end of morality, and the coming of an age of perplexity and violence. God is dead in man's heart and experience; and, added Nietzsche, 'As yet no new God lies in cradle and swaddling clothes.' He thus carried scepticism to its final destination, which is nihilism – the belief that nothing remains.

Nietzsche could not laugh about this situation. Christianity cannot lightly be abandoned. It was not like belief in Father Christmas, a mere tale, of no vital relevance to living. Christianity had been our food and nourishment for over 1,000 years. Nietzsche rather was acutely pained by the absence of God, for he saw its awful implications.

He told another and more famous parable in an earlier work, *The Gay Science*. A madman carrying a lantern goes into a market-place one bright morning crying incessantly, 'I am looking for God.' The crowd are unconcerned and eye him complacently. 'Have you lost him then?' says one; 'Did he lose his way like a child?' says another. But he cries out: 'Where has God gone? I shall tell you. We have killed him – you and I. ... Is not more and more night coming on all the time? Is not the greatness of this deed too great for us?' The loiterers do not understand, but remain silent and astonished. The madman throws his lantern to the ground. 'I come too early. My time has not yet come. This tremendous event is still on its way.'

It was not easy for Nietzsche to be an atheist, for he understood the implications deeply. While the optimists of his day were indulging in confident speculations about the future of man at last freed from the bondage of religion, Nietzsche was one of the very few to see what departure from the Christian faith might really mean. And Nietzsche alone could say in the golden days of the 1880s: 'We have entered the classical age of war.'

But there is another aspect to Nietzsche's atheism. With that almost terrifying sense of emptiness due to the absence of God in his experience, he combines an intense dislike of Christianity. Perhaps this was a form of extreme reaction against the oppressiveness of his upbringing. At times in his writings, and especially in his later work *The Antichrist*, he almost presents us with a direct antithesis to the yearning of some of the Victorians who would have said, 'We cannot honestly believe in God but we would like to.' Nietzsche comes near to saying, 'Even if God does exist we must kill him, for belief in God is crippling the human race.' This attitude of deliberate dislike for Christianity is not consistent with the other, of mourning for a lost God, but in it Nietzsche has anticipated an attitude often found today. His reasons for it are worth exploring.

He held that the Christian categories are an illusion. The Christian faith consists, he said, of imaginary causes – sin, the Fall; imaginary beings – God, the Redeemer;

imaginary effects – salvation and forgiveness. Thus the Christian faith leads men into a world of make-believe with no point of contact with reality. This is worse even than dreaming, for dreams at least do act as mirrors of reality. For Nietzsche the Christian concepts had no accompanying experience, no existential reality, and so were meaningless.

But more than that, Nietzsche believed that the flight into the world of religion was due to a sickness of the soul. The whole apparatus of theology is really a projection of states of the nervous system – morbid states. It comes from a fear and hatred of reality. 'The inner world of the religious man looks exactly like the inner world of the over-excited and the exhausted.' Furthermore, where Christianity finds men healthy it makes them sick by giving them a sense of guilt and failure. Then it can bring a fictitious sense of redemption. Faith, according to Nietzsche, does not move mountains; it puts mountains where there were none.

Thus, with its cowardly and petty values, Christianity is the great destroyer of life. Its work is not to liberate, as it claims, but to bind and destroy. Historically it cheated the world of the harvest of ancient culture, pagan and Islamic. Today it deprives men of fullness of life by condemning as sinful man's most rich and full-blooded pleasures. In his wilder passages Nietzsche cursed Paul as the man who took a sect within Judaism (where it might have remained harmless for ever), and turned it into a potential world religion able to damage millions. He professed to dislike the whole atmosphere of the New Testament, in which the only character he praised was Pilate, for his Roman scorn and indifference.

So in *The Antichrist* he conceives of 'parasitism as the only practice of the church, with its ideal of anaemia, of draining all the blood, all love, all hope for life . . . the cross as the mark of recognition for the most subterranean conspiracy that ever existed – against health, beauty, whatever has turned out well, courage, spirit, graciousness of the soul, against life itself!' And in *Thus Spoke Zarathustra* he complains, 'He whom they call Redeemer has cast them into bondage. . . . Ah that someone would redeem them from their Redeemer.'

God is dead. This is a statement of the experience both of Nietzche himself and of many people in the generations that have followed him. The Christian faith is a morbid illusion. This is really a psychological criticism, strikingly similar to the claim made by Freud some years later that religion is a form of chronic mental illness, based on the craving for ultimate security. Faith is the refuge of the weak. This idea, too, has become widely accepted. Very few contemporary images of the strong, the free, the successful, or the truly human person would allow him any dependence on religion.

The later existentialists, notably Sartre, reared in an intellectual climate that was further removed from Christian piety, do not seem to have the qualms that atheism caused Nietzsche, especially in his earlier years. God is definitely dead for them, and under no circumstances do they want him back. Nietzsche was haunted by the emptiness which the death of God had caused. His successors generally accept it as a datum.

## Life is meaningless

Nietzsche, although he had become an atheist, still believed that God was the source of all significance. But God had died, and with him all meaning had vanished from the earth. The Christian idea of a meaningful existence whose ultimate aim is the service of God, and the whole Christian system of morality based on God's law, collapse if God is no more. Nietzsche is again making a statement about his own experience of life, which he believed would become true for many besides himself.

In his parable about the madman in the market-place, the people in the crowd are scornfully indifferent when they hear of the death of God. They continue as if nothing were altered. But the madman, whom in some sense we must identify with Nietzsche himself, believes that nothing can be the same again. 'Are we not perpetually falling? Backward, sideward, forward in all directions? Is there any up or down left? Are we not straying through an infinite nothing?' Though his own age was blind to it, Nietzsche believed that the heart and soul had already gone from Western civilization.

Nietzsche's parable seems to have been verified in the history of this century. Certainly his pessimism has been much nearer the mark than the hopeful fancies of the rationalists who were his contemporaries, as we can see clearly now, some eighty years after he wrote. Although Christian worship and Christian values have by no means disappeared, there has been a widespread departure from formal Christianity and a widespread rejection of Christian morals. Western society now faces a crisis of values, because without Christianity there seem to be no clear criteria for deciding right and wrong. It is true that the 'permissive society' sometimes means a society that shows more compassion. But this phrase also stands for the fact that we are living in an ethical vacuum, a society that knows almost no restraints because it has no means of deciding what they should be. Inevitably this is a time of disillusionment and protest, especially for those born since the end of the war. It is not easy to live without a moral structure.

There are really two consequences from 'God is dead' in Nietzsche's thinking. First, there is no ultimate meaning or purpose to be found within life itself. Second, the moral values that derived from belief in God are no more; there is now not even a basis for morality. So Nietzsche wrote: 'What is nihilism? The fact that the highest values lose all value. There is no aim, no answer to the question "Why?" Man has lost all dignity in his own eyes.'

Nietzche himself is inconsistent in his attitude, rather as he is in his attitude to the death of God. At one moment the meaninglessness of life causes him almost unbearable anguish, and at another he demolishes the Christian way with spite and gusto. Zarathustra sees his hearers shrinking back in dismay at his nihilistic teaching, unable as yet to bear it: 'Do you flee from me? Are you frightened? Do you tremble at this saying?' But he is also able to cry out, about the Christian moral code: 'O my brothers, shatter, shatter the old law-tables, shatter, shatter, the good and the just.'

It is the first of these, the attitude of anxiety, that is most characteristic of existential thinking. Once a person genuinely believes that life is meaningless, everything is changed. The universe, however vast the astronomers show it to be, is still a homely place for those who believe in a God whose presence pervades it all; but it is a place of terrifying loneliness for those to whom God is dead. This is why Nietzsche speaks of the 'great terror, the great prospect, the great sickness, the great disgust, the great sea-sickness' in the quotation with which this section began. Perhaps it was this terror which finally drove him to insanity.

Nietzsche uses a telling metaphor to describe the meaninglessness of life. When a person comes to feel that God is dead it is as if he has come to the brink of a great abyss, whose unfathomable darkness fills him with terror. The firm land of Christian morality is finished, and now there lies before him an infinite nothing. Peering over the edge, it is not surprising that he feels a terrible unease, a sort of spiritual vertigo. In Nietzsche's view it would have been cowardice to retreat from the abyss back into the comfort of belief. Yet the abyss is so daunting that it fills him with acute anxiety, almost to the point of despair and self-destruction.

'Life is meaningless', besides being a very common feeling in the post-war world, is a recurrent theme in modern literature. We must now look at the way in which three modern authors have expressed it. The first, from Sartre's first novel, *La Nausée*, will be in some detail, because on this topic it is possibly the classic passage in all existentialist writing.

This book takes the form of the diary of a man named Roquentin. The total of external events described is very small, because the author wants us to concentrate on the inner world of Roquentin's thought and emotion. There are times when Roquentin feels that life has no meaning at all, and that the very fact that he exists is absurd. This gives him a sense of uneasiness and disgust which at times comes near to overpowering him.

One day, while he is in a municipal park, the nausea comes upon him. He feels that he has no reason at all for existing; that he is superfluous. He thinks vaguely about killing himself, but realizes that his death would be pointless too. So he comes to perceive that the starting-point in his thinking about life must be the very meaninglessness of it. 'I understood that I had found the key to Existence, the key to my nausea, to my own life. In fact, all that I was able to grasp afterwards comes down to this fundamental absurdity.'

He sees a tree blossoming, but in this mood has no eye for its beauty. 'Existence everywhere, to infinity, superfluous, always and everywhere.' He ponders on the fact that the tree will die. And then he gives the statement which perhaps sums up better than any other the existentialist attitude to life: 'Every existent is born without reason, prolongs itself out of weakness, and dies by chance.' He concludes about the tree: 'There were no reasons for it to exist . . . but it was not possible for it not to exist.' Applying this to the human predicament, he is saying that we can find within life no possible meaning or purpose, but we cannot escape the fact that we do exist. Life is meaningless, but it must be lived.

This episode in Sartre's first novel is an anticipation of his own journey of thought. For when he came to writing serious philosophy, the starting-point of his own system was 'this fundamental absurdity'. Sartre the philosopher has not been so successful as Sartre the novelist and playwright. In his major work *L'Etre et le Néant*, he attempted to produce a whole framework based on the concept of negation. The world is revealed to us by negation, the sense of being other than, separate from, objects and other people. Negation prevails in the dealings of human beings with one another. A fellow-human being is not so much a friend or brother as a rival and an enemy, whose interests conflict with mine. I am bound therefore to reduce him to the level of an object and make use of him, lest he make use of me.

The sense of Nothing, according to Sartre, is our most fundamental experience. But when he comes to construct an elaborate edifice of theory based on Nothing, using a metaphysics which many would consider archaic, he falls an easy prey for the linguistic analysts. It is simple to demonstrate that, according to modern linguistic criteria, many of his philosophical statements are without meaning. But in his plays and novels Sartre's presentation of the futility of life and the beastliness of man to man communicates itself much more readily. Perhaps one reason why the existentialists are so widely read and understood is the fact that they have frequently offered their ideas, not in conceptual form, but in imagery and concrete situations.

A second example from modern literature is Franz Kafka's novel *The Trial*. This is the story of a man who one day suddenly finds that he is arraigned on a charge about which he knows nothing. He is subjected to the bewildering processes of a court which never actually confronts him, and before which he is never allowed to defend himself. He can discover how his case is progressing only through unreliable rumours, though he is repeatedly given to understand that it is going against him. His internal security and his efficiency at his job are gradually undermined. In the end he is taken away one night and a knife is thrust into his heart.

This weird story, nightmarish in the way that details are so vivid yet the whole so perplexing, gives a different view of the meaninglessness of life. Man seems to be at times in the grip of strange forces which, though scarcely apprehended, have an irresistible compulsion. They threaten his existence and may even destroy him. In *The Trial*, the accused tries to keep a clear head and understand his situation coolly. But that is what he finds he is never able to do, because he is never given enough information.

Why should this strange court exist and why should this man's 'case' come up for trial? Possibly Kafka is dealing in an oblique way with the basic human problem of guilt which, though apparently without objective basis, can be a crushing and destructive burden. It is even possible to feel guilty for existing. Those whose circumstances are insecure or unhappy are particularly liable to a sense of existential guilt. A number of the existentialists, it seems, have had to endure a heavy load; in the case of Nietzsche, possibly the aftermath of an oppressive and unbalanced upbringing; in the case of Kafka, the insecurity of being a displaced and sometimes unwanted person. What they have suffered in an acute form, most people may have to face at some time or to some degree. It is a basic part of human experience which they have brought painfully to light.

Albert Camus, whose name was for a time popularly coupled with that of Sartre, is another writer deeply affected by the apparent meaninglessness of life, though his mood is less introverted and nihilistic. One of his novels, *The Plague*, treats this theme in an almost allegorical way. It is the story of an epidemic of plague, so serious that the town in which it occurs has to be closed to the outside world. The novel records the progress of the disease and the various reactions of the citizens daily face to face with death, under the stress of constant uncertainty. The plague is no respecter of persons and its comings and goings are quite unpredictable.

Camus is using this to portray the struggle of human beings against a meaningless life, in which sorrow and disaster seem to come without regard to human desert or merit. While the struggle is often heroic and unselfish, it is clear that man can never be more than a temporary victor, for although the plague may subside, the bacillus never dies or disappears for ever. Having remained quiescent for years it comes again, as destructive as it was before. When man has done the best he can, life still will be too cruel, too powerful, too unmanageable for him to have the final victory. Camus dissociated himself from the name of existentialism, but in this novel has much in common with the existentialist attitude. As one of his characters puts it: 'But what does that mean – "plague"? Just life, no more than that.'

An emptiness, a dark abyss, a meaningless trial, a plague; anxiety due to life's futility, anxiety due to a sense of guilt, anxiety because we have to die. This is the general existentialist verdict about human life, often made as a result of personal suffering. Nietzsche saw the emptiness as due to the death of God. For most of those who follow him, meaninglessness is simply a fundamental truth about our existence, which must be faced if there is to be any hope of a constructive solution.

## Man becomes God

Life is meaningless, said Nietzsche, since God is dead. Yet because mankind must have a God upon whom to rely, and from whom to receive its values, there seems to be only one answer. Man must himself occupy the place of God, and take upon himself the roles formerly attributed to the deity. Since he can no longer turn to an outside source of help he must now find within his own personality the power to live. Making his own judgments, coming to decisions without external guidance, forming his own values, he must create his own meaning for life.

Nietzsche realized that this was an exceedingly difficult task; he looked forward to the man who would do it fully, and called him the superman. But before he can come, conventional belief and morality must be displaced; which is the reason why, in the story of the tightrope walker, the buffoon has to push off the man in front of him as he takes the perilous path forward. So Zarathustra announces: 'Behold I teach you the superman . . . the superman shall be the meaning of the earth.'

It is hard, now, not to be prejudiced against the word 'superman'. It has been much misunderstood, largely because the writings of Nietzsche were used in a way that did violence to their meaning, and were unscrupulously enlisted in support of causes which he himself repudiated. With a writer so impassioned and unguarded it was easy to extract passages from their context and use them to uphold such antisocial doctrines as anti-Semitism or the Aryan master-race.

In German the word is *Übermensch*; literally, 'over-man'. It is Nietzsche's ideal of a man who can overcome the gravest problems of life, including the anxiety of the abyss. He is big enough, and God-like enough, to give life meaning. He is powerful, creative and courageous.

He delights in the richness of life, exulting in the body and fulfilling its desires. His laughter is free and full, even though his life may be both tragic and profound: 'I love him whose soul is deep even in its ability to be wounded.' He enjoys the wealth of culture and learning, but his thinking, unlike that of the dry intellectual, is passionate and committed. He holds his convictions that they may lead to action. Nietzsche hated pettiness and meanness: 'It is not your sin, but your moderation that cries to heaven. Your very meanness in sinning cries to heaven!' So the superman is lavish and generous in all his deeds. He is also totally irreligious, because he is strong enough to be an atheist and bear the consequent anxiety.

There is no place in Nietzsche's philosophy for the 'greatest happiness of the greatest number', which is a despicable ideal for all absolute existentialists. The superman, because he is supremely an individualist, will always stand out against the dullness, mediocrity, and cowardice of the crowd. Nietzsche did, however, allow him the possibility of friendship: 'I teach you the friend and the overflowing heart . . . I teach you the friend in whom the world stands complete, a vessel of the good, the creative friend who has a world to bestow'; words strangely like those of Buber.

This, then, is Nietzsche's concept of the superman: a noble but almost barbaric figure who combines great intellectual and creative talents with courage and physical strength. He will conquer the masses and, far more significant, even the fate which may sometimes turn against him. The contrast between Nietzsche the man, timid, weak, inhibited, and the ideal which he puts forward is so glaring that one cannot avoid feeling in some respects that the superman was what Nietzsche was not, but in fantasy wished he might be. There is undoubtedly a resemblance between the superman and certain modern ultra-heroes such as James Bond. For this we must make allowance, because it is Nietzsche's personal compensation.

At the deepest level, I believe that we are being offered a psychological ideal. For the superman is the free man. Religion, Nietzsche would say, has made men into slaves by suppressing the great drives within them. What the psychologists call aggression Nietzsche called the will to power. This he believed had often been held back when it should be allowed free expression. He placed the blame directly on the Christian faith, which by exalting humility and meekness among its virtues had given its adherents a servile mentality. The other great drive, sex, he also believed had been dangerously inhibited, so that 'many of the outwardly chaste have filth at the bottom of their souls'. The superman, however, has been liberated. His inner drives are no longer held back to frustration, but released creatively into life.

The main role of the superman, to which we must now return, is his giving a meaning to life. How this is achieved is hinted at in Zarathustra's first words to the people: 'I teach you the superman. Man is something that should be overcome.' He must rise above the common level, and become the man over himself. His self-overcoming is a much profounder thing than self-control as conceived by traditional morality; it is a conquest of that deepest personal anxiety which lies at the roots of our being-in-the-world.

We have already seen how the meaninglessness of life caused Nietzsche to tremble when he realized that he must stand alone, and how he likened this to a dark abyss. The overcoming man is able to find a way not of escape from the abyss, but beyond it. 'He possesses heart who knows fear, but masters fear; who sees the abyss, but sees it with pride. He who sees the abyss but with an eagle's eyes – he who grasps the abyss with an eagle's claws; he possesses courage.' Nietzsche's solution, then, is to see the abyss and grasp it. What exactly does this mean?

It means courageously to accept the fact that life has no meaning; to be honest; to look the fact full in the face and not to flinch; to abandon all hopes that it is otherwise; and to cast away all illusions of security. This in itself is an act of great courage, which is bound to be preceded by something near despair. But the overcoming man must bear the anxiety in full, for only by taking it upon himself can he hope to overcome it. It is, in fact, to admit that one has to have the role of God, and to accept this is the most responsible task of all.

Then, one has to choose for oneself how to live. This too is an anguishing thing to do, because one is at that point master of one's own destiny, and making a decision without any guiding principles at all. The choice must be absolutely personal, with no reference to the advice or help of others. Though terrifying, it has to be done if a man is ever truly to live. It is even better to choose that which leads to disaster than not to choose at all. The superman is the free man, and this is the essence of his freedom, that he has had the courage to decide for himself alone. That is why, much later, Sartre wrote: 'Total responsibility in total solitude – is not this the very definition of liberty?'

So man becomes God. In religious thought God is the cause beyond whom there is no further cause; there can be no enquiry beyond him; he is totally unconditioned. Now man must take all that upon himself, and become his own foundation of meaning and value. One man may become a freedom-fighter, another a sadist and another a saint. Each is answerable only to himself, and is therefore, like God, beyond criticism. The man who thus grasps the abyss and finds his freedom is the superman.

Nietzsche presents these ideas in an almost mythological form, in which lasting insights are mingled inseparably with fantasy and excess. The saner aspects of his doctrine of the superman, however, contain the germ of almost all later existential thinking. Martin Heidegger's expression of it is similar. He too uses the metaphor of the abyss in talking about man's predicament. He teaches that when a person understands, and accepts that life is meaningless, he comes to a new understanding of himself. If he can face it, and make his own personal responsible choice, he passes from nonentity into 'authentic existence', where he is no longer a slave to forces outside himself, such as social conformity, popular opinion, or conventional ideas of success. He enters a new liberty in which he is truly responsible for his actions and opinions, and is unafraid to stand alone.

It is true, of course, that our mastery of our fate is limited, because the past is immutably fixed. But existentialism asserts that by the attitude we adopt, even to our past, we are able to transform it. It is sheer weakness to admit that we are totally the products of our upbringing or heredity or present circumstances. Existentialism seeks to break the chain of causation, and insists that individually we are able to make ourselves. 'I choose myself, not in my being, but in my manner of being', wrote Sartre. In other words, I cannot choose the fact that I am here, now. But what I make of this situation is entirely my own.

In some existential thinking these ideas are extended to include another important concept – commitment. When man asserts his freedom in making a choice he is not giving assent to an academic idea; he is staking his life and future. Thus to choose between, say, communism and capitalism means nothing until one becomes involved in one or the other, until either one throws one's lot whole-heartedly in with the Communist Party, or one invests all one's money in a capitalist-run business.

Kierkegaard, a century ago, clearly perceived this in his own religious terms. The choice to follow Christ means nothing, he said, until in utter faith one has leapt out into the unknown, totally committed to obedience with no possibility of going back. Abraham's commitment was measured by his willingness even to take a knife to his son when he believed God had commanded it, though the doing of it meant unbearable anguish.

Sartre found the idea of commitment verified in his own experience during the second world war. After being a prisoner in Germany for a year, he was released on grounds of ill health and went back to France which was then occupied by the Germans. There he took an active part in the *Résistance*. In this exciting and perilous work Sartre found his own form of authentic existence. He had made a true existential commitment because his activities might well have cost him his life. Yet, paradoxically, by throwing in his lot against the Germans he was asserting his personal freedom, for he was no longer a slave to the dictates of the oppressor. Freedom in existential terms means something like 'the power to take decisions completely alone and utterly without compulsion'. During the years of the occupation the choice and the commitment were repeated in day after day of dangerous living. Of this time and of the men with whom he worked Sartre wrote: 'Each of them, standing against the oppressor undertook to be himself, freely and irrevocably.' To become and to be oneself, that is everything.

Commitment is very difficult for the true existentialist, because it might involve working with other people and so forfeiting personal independence. To join a movement or embrace a cause, positively, is to risk enslavement. It is committing the sin of 'seriousness' and becoming less than a man. Perhaps the form of commitment that suits existentialism best is that to a movement of resistance or revolt, because this emphasizes that negation on which the whole view of life is based. The commitment is therefore, typically, a standing against and, best of all, an individual protest. The desperate sacrifice of the Czeck student who burnt himself to death after the Russian intervention in his country epitomizes the existential idea of commitment. It was the definitive act by which, though it cost him his life, he authenticated himself.

Sartre claimed for existentialism that it is a 'humanism', meaning a sane and practicable way of life based on the truth about our predicament, unpalatable though that may be. Of what, then, does this way consist? It is not easy to answer because existentialism is so fragmentary, but if a general pattern emerges, it is this. A human being, according to existentialism, must pass through the sequence of experiences: dread at the meaninglessness of life; the brink of despair; facing the situation; making a deliberate choice; commitment; and so into authentic existence. This has a certain similarity to Christian conversion, but it has an unashamedly nihilistic starting-point. Also, though there can be a heroic struggle, there is no hope of ultimate victory or reconciliation. While this may seem a harsh philosophy, it professes to be a courageous one; and though it lacks an over-all structure, it claims to be more true to our real situation than any system developed by reason and urged forward by optimistic hopes.

## The way of self-destruction

Existentialism has become influential because it has commended itself as relevant to the modern situation. The glowing optimism of the nineteenth century has vanished for ever, and now even the humanists themselves express their hopes more soberly. Very few people today will claim for science what was claimed 100 years ago, that it is the key to all progress. We know too well that besides bringing enormous benefits it has become the potential destroyer of our race. The old, comfortable, predictable order of things in the Western world is breaking or has broken. Existentialism speaks authentically to the bewilderment that has ensued.

In the face of the violence and destruction that have come upon us this century, a philosophy based on the fundamental goodness of man seems altogether naïve. That is why, as we have seen, humanism often appears inadequate. But existentialism, though dark and pessimistic, does at least deal with the realities of human life. It takes proper account both of the conflict between human personalities, and of our fundamental selfishness. It deals more truly with our inner world, because though it may have little to say about happiness, it is fully aware of that anxiety and dread and loneliness which are frequently the human lot. Existentialism talks of man in a way which we find true to personal experience. Whether the solution offered by Sartre and others is adequate is a different matter, but they are at least speaking in meaningful terms.

The stress given by existentialism to the place of the individual has been most needed. We live today in larger and larger aggregates in which it is hard to find personal expression. Our food and clothes are mass-produced; our houses and flats may even look very much the same; the State and the Health Service and their impersonal agents the computers, in order to deal with large numbers, tend to treat people as mere digits. All this and more has depersonalized our existence. Existentialism has asserted again the need for individuality, and by insisting that no-one need be the slave of the forces that impinge upon him, has been a challenge to many to find a truly personal way of life.

With increased prosperity our society has generally adopted very materialistic values. We have become acquisitive. Many of the prime motivations of today are towards wealth and promotion, however unsatisfying these have been found to be in themselves. Existentialism, however, has insisted that personal experience and personal commitment are the true stuff of life. It has issued a warning to a world so intent on getting and doing that it has forgotten simply how to be.

In these and other ways existentialism has been a necessary corrective to the scientific approach to life. If it has been an extreme reaction, perhaps that is because exaggerated claims were made for science also. The general approach to life which the existential method involves cannot be neglected if we are to do justice to our humanity and inwardness.

But existentialism is more than a methodology. While the value of the existential method would be denied by very few, the general philosophy of existentialism as put forward by Nietzsche and his successors has serious weaknesses.[3]

At the outset, however, let it be remembered that it is easy to make facile objections to minor weaknesses in the writings of the existentialists, and to fail to hear their real message. The frequent exaggerations, the inconsistencies, the undeveloped ideas, the use of dramatic situations, render them an easy prey for the critics. Nietzsche is the most vulnerable of all. It is not difficult to pick on his more fantastic notions, his apparent violence and racialism, in order to discredit him. But this is to miss the point. The main theses of existentialism must be assessed, not the superficialities. From an absolute existentialist standpoint there can of course be no criticism because there are no criteria. But for those who allow reason a certain validity these two criticisms must be offered.

First, by stressing the personal so much existentialism

[3] For a humanist critique see H. Hawton, *The Feast of Unreason* (Rationalist Press).

has become a philosophy of extreme subjectivism, and as such is open to great abuses. The absence of any outside frame of reference by which a man's actions may be judged means that any form of conduct, however irresponsible or antisocial, can be justified. Nietzsche held that the departure of Christianity from the Western world would mean that there would be no moral code at all. Man then becomes God and everyone is a law unto himself. It is a short step from there to letting everyone do exactly as he wants without regard to the effects on other people. If I have made an appointment with someone, and I suddenly decide I have something better to do such as going to the cinema, I follow my desire. If I see my neighbour's diamond ring and I want it and am cunning or powerful enough to get it, then I do so. Those who apply existentialism in this sort of way do not have to justify their conduct to anyone. They have only to please themselves.

Existentialism lays a very necessary stress on experience; but this can easily be distorted into the proposition that experience is the all-important thing, an idea which can be both dangerous and degrading. For example, since some of the most intense forms of experience are sexual, the cult of experience can easily become the cult of sex, pursued not as part of the responsible commitment of one person to another, nor even as the expression of a more casual affection. As a modern sexologist, Dr Kronhausen, has put it: 'People should enjoy sex for itself alone.' The experience becomes more important than the persons involved. Hence the interest in some modern literature is often not so much in sexual love as in all forms of sexual experience including the most bizarre and outlandish. But thus depersonalized, sex has lost its most human aspect.

Furthermore, for those who feel that their inner world is the most important thing, taking drugs is not only permissible but to be commended. When that world is bleak and colourless, a 'trip' may provide a temporary excitement. The harmful effect of some drugs is incontrovertible; but even where drug-taking has caused a person no measurable damage to mind or body, it has drawn his attention away from the real human world of work and recreation and relationship. The cult of the inner environment is not truly personal. And anyone who is being mentally or physically injured by drugs may justly reply to his critics, according to the principles of existentialism: 'It is my own affair if it destroys me. My life is my own; I make my own choice; I carry the responsibility myself.'

The 'hippies' may therefore be regarded as the practical outworking of a form of the existentialist creed. What appears to be in many ways a laudable revolt against the materialism and lovelessness of society, has led many to a life of drifting and futility. The quest for experience as an end in itself almost always ends in disillusionment and frustration.

The existentialist way, it may be argued, is so subjective that it unfits human beings for living in community together, though they must so live. True existentialism sees men as so isolated that friendship is a meaningless term, and even sexual love, in common thought held to be the profoundest expression of union between two people, is an arrangement for mutual satisfaction or even for mutual sadism. Yet it is plain that human personality only takes shape and grows to maturity through human relationships. Existentialism, in denying the possibility of true relationship, denies the most human thing about us.

Existentialism interpreted thus is the philosophy of complete selfishness, because it refuses to allow any interest other than self-interest. It is doubly dangerous when a nation or political party comes to make itself into God. It can then justify all forms of oppression. We live with the spectre of the gas-chambers

in which millions of Jews were exterminated; of geno-
cide; of apartheid; of thought-control by brain-
washing. Yet all these things are consistent with a form
of existentialism. Though Nietzsche himself would have
been horrified, it was easy for the Nazis to use his
writings to give a sort of apostolic authority to their
atrocities.

Existentialism must be criticized for a second reason.
Its extreme pessimism is not true to common experience.
A number of the existentialist writers appear to have
been abnormally sensitive and in some cases near the
border of mental sickness, which means that the view of
life which they impart is distorted. Certain aspects of our
existence, fear, guilt, and despair, are portrayed with a
skill that is unsurpassed; other aspects such as love and
hope are neglected altogether. The existentialists have
an incomparable sense of the sorriness and tragedy of
human existence, but their experience is one-sided.
They are thus not qualified to offer a whole philosophy
of life.

The most destructive feature of existentialism is the
assertion that life has no meaning or purpose. Man seems
to have deep within his psyche a craving for order and
intelligibility in the world around him. He has commonly sought for meaning through two channels –
religion and scientific enquiry. Existentialism denies
them both.

The thought of life having no meaning at all can
cause acute anxiety, and for a very sensitive person this
may become intolerable. Nietzsche spoke of 'grasping
the abyss', of honestly admitting that life has no meaning. He tried to do so himself, and went mad. His
insanity may have had other factors behind it, but we
cannot avoid the impression that he created for himself
a view of life that he could not bear. A frail person in
any case, he cut himself off from any possible source of
comfort and stability, and was destroyed by the violence

of his own ideas. There have been many others who, on reaching the same conclusions about life, have despaired and either broken down or killed themselves. Suicide is a form of personal commitment that, according to existentialism, is completely justified.

Existentialism proposes a way of liberation. It requires man to take the place of God. But that role man is not big enough to play, because the responsibility of being what Sartre called 'the unfounded foundation of all values' is too crushing. It may be that the only one who can adequately take that role is God himself.

It is one thing to play with existentialism as an intellectual game without taking it really seriously, or to find in it an excuse for abandoning moral restraints. But to treat it existentially, to accept its propositions as a way of life, is quite another. Fortunately, perhaps, there are few healthy people who take it as seriously as that. For the majority it remains an academic exercise, a sea in which to paddle but not to swim. Though it purports to be a philosophy of courageous living, very few in practice live by it. Existentialism offers insights which are of the utmost relevance, but a total view of life which must be condemned. Judged even by experience, the only evidence it admits, it is not fully human.

'A man is only a man when he is like God and lives in fellowship with him.' Stephen Neill.

'To come into the field of force of God's infinite caring is to feel ... unlimited liability for one another.' Douglas Steere.

Existentialism and rational humanism, while radically opposed in many respects, do at least have one thing in common: their total rejection of religion in its usual theistic sense. The non-existence of God is the practical starting-point of humanism; it is also the basic experience from which existentialism has grown.

Although Christianity accepts a number of insights from both, it has a totally different starting-point. A first-century writer defending Christianity in comparison with the secular philosophies of his day advised his readers: 'Shake off the hidebound notions which can only lead to error, and put yourself in the position of a brand-new man on the point of hearing a brand-new language.'[1] Christianity has always involved an unfamiliar way of thinking which comes strangely to those who throughout their intellectual training have lived with the assumption that there is no God. It does so still today. We must understand at the outset why the Christian approach is so different.

Humanism and existentialism are man-made systems of thought; they claim nothing more. But Christianity purports to be God's self-declaration. If God is

[1] *The Letter to Diognetus.*

infinite, man by himself can never find him. God must reveal himself. This claim for Christianity may seem laughable in view of the endless wranglings between Christians of different denominations. It may reasonably be claimed, however, that there is an essential Christian religion that has existed right from the days when the New Testament was written. It has been present in the Christian church ever since, despite a great variety of outward expressions and the fact that at some periods parts of the church have deviated far from the basic faith. The authentic Christianity is that of the Bible, in which there is a record of God gradually revealing himself to the Jews until they had a sufficient understanding, and then his ultimate self-declaration in Jesus Christ. That, at any rate, is the Christian claim.

It is natural, therefore, that there should be an element of dogmatism in statements of Christian belief, which is not present, or should not be, in non-religious philosophy. But if God has indeed revealed himself, a note of authority is altogether reasonable. The possibility that this is so must at least be allowed as a prerequisite for an honest examination of Christianity. Then, as with the other two views of man which we have considered, the Christian one must be looked at whole before it is judged.

Christianity thus involves a reversal of the secular starting-point, and a denial of many secular assertions. The critics of religion tend to say that belief in God is a prop for the immature or insecure, an illusion grown from wish-fulfilment. That sort of remark has been made as easily by Bertrand Russell as by Friedrich Nietzsche. But the Christian holds that God, far from being an illusion, is the reality from whom all truth originates. Therefore in Christian understanding any attempt to build a life for man which ignores God cannot in the long run succeed or satisfy. What the atheist considers to be an unnecessary, indeed an imaginary, prop, the Christian sees as an integral part of the structure. A thoroughgoing atheist looks down on the man who prays as immature, abnormal, maimed. But the Christian holds that it is the man who refuses to believe who is immature.

One further caution must be given. The Christian religion is not, fundamentally, a structure of theoretical ideas. Its assertions are generally founded upon experience; of a succession of men who believed God had spoken to them; and from those who were with Jesus when he lived and died. Whether the Christian interpretation is correct is for the reader to judge. But it must be remembered that religious language can never be separated from experience. It speaks of things which, though they lie beyond the possibility of accurate definition, are apprehended by the whole person. Some religious statements therefore may appear to be indirect or metaphorical. In theology, it has been truly said, we can only babble and mutter. Yet there are those who claim to know Theos, the subject of all theology, with a conviction that goes beyond the reach of words. It is the understanding of man which comes from that conviction with which we have to deal.

## Existence with meaning

Man is God's creation. The Christian understanding of man must begin here. According to Christianity, man is not just a collection of chemicals that came into being by an intricate process and then evolved mind and consciousness. Man owes his whole being, his physical vitality and his spiritual aspirations, to God from whom all life derives. His existence is no chance or accident.

The early chapters of Genesis describe creation in evocative pictorial language, more akin to poetry than science. The whole natural order, the primaeval energy, the earth, the sea, the plants, the animals, and finally man himself, are declared to be the work of God, and good. God is described as forming man from dust and breathing into him, giving him life. That is to say, it is God who has designed man to be what he is: thinker, artist, scientist, builder; above all, worshipper. Man's enormous creative capacity comes from the Creator. The most creative act of all is a response to him. That, as Christians understand it, is why men of every race and culture seem to feel for God, even when the expression of their search is crude and superstitious.

The Christian doctrine of creation is not concerned with the biological details of man's origin. That is the proper field of study for the zoologist and anthropologist. But Christianity does assert that by whatever means man has come into being, it is the work of God. The theory of evolution is at present generally considered to be the best description of the development of living things that science can give, though like all scientific theories, it is open to criticism and will need modification as new evidence comes to light. But at best it is only a description of the process. The belief of Christians is that, whatever the process, the author is God. It would be a misunderstanding, incidentally, to think that creation by a process is less divine than a series of mighty acts that do it all at once.

Science describes processes and relates apparently unrelated facts, but its accounts are always incomplete, for they can never in the ultimate sense be explanations. Genesis, however, purports to be an explanation of man's existence, not in terms of science but of meaning, by referring it to God's creative act.

Man was formed by God. Genesis also teaches that he was made in the image of God; he bears a reproduction of some of God's characteristics. This means, first, that man has a capacity for love and self-giving. The theologians have long pondered over the question, Why did God bring his creation into being at all, if he is self-sufficient and in need of no other? The beginning of an answer can be given by analogy with love between a man and a woman. Though there is the deepest satisfaction in their love, they wish it to overflow into having children who will be both the fruit and the object of their love. So also, perhaps, it is with God. The creation was the overflowing of his love.

A human analogy has been used here, but really the analogy is the other way round. It is man whose creative love reflects that of God. Though pale and weak by comparison, and never entirely freed from self-interest, human love can have some of the quality of true self-giving. There was no common word in the ancient world for this kind of love. That presumably is why the early Christians had to take the word *agapē* and give it a new meaning of their own.

Man's capacity for love and self-giving must be used, in response to other human beings and above all in response to God. Existentialism denies that this is possible. But according to Christianity not only is it possible; it is the great task of life.

'In God's image' means, second, that man has a will of his own. Returning to the analogy of human love, we may say that no parents would want a child who was a machine with unalterable fixed reactions, even if those reactions were of total obedience. One thing is certain: the reactions could never be those of love. No-one can be conditioned to love, for love is the free response of an independent will and can only be voluntary. So if we are indeed the creation of God, it is reasonable that we should have our own autonomy. He has given us the power either to respond to him or to turn away. Man, says Genesis, was placed in a garden where he was free. Round the forbidden tree there was no electric fence. Though man could give all love and obedience freely, he was also free to eat the fruit and reject the authority of God. In the Christian view, the abuse of this freedom is the fundamental error of mankind.

Third, it means that man has a position of authority, under God and over the rest of the creation. All authority derives from God, but some is delegated to man to whom so many talents are entrusted. He is given the commission to become master of the world. He is expected to find out the potentialities of earth, air and sea, to use nature and its resources. He is required to give names to all living creatures. In this we can see the scientific quest foreshadowed, whose aim is to understand and classify the natural world. Here is the divine charter for the immense variety of human activity: agriculture, technology, industry, craft and art. These, according to Christianity, are God's gifts for the enrichment of man's life.

But authority can be misused. If science and technology have not turned out to be an unmitigated blessing it is not because the pursuit of them is unworthy, but because they have often been used godlessly, without care or compassion. Polluted atmospheres, man-made deserts, nuclear stock-piles and many other blights on our environment are the direct result of human selfishness and greed. When man exerts his authority without reference to God he does so at his peril. For though in authority he is still a creature and, as Christians see it, to usurp the place of God is the crowning folly.

If the Christian understanding of man as God's creation, in God's image, is true, it means that man's life has both meaning and purpose. Nietzsche the atheist held that all meaning, all significance, comes from God. Christians believe that too, but they also believe in God. Man finds his meaning in God. This would certainly explain why it is that, when he tries to live his life apart from God, he discovers it to be meaningless, as Nietzsche so tragically realized. The poignancy of so much existentialist writing is that it describes exactly what would be expected if men who are made in the image of God deny him and try to live on their own.

What, then, is the meaning and the purpose in the Christian view? The meaning is love. Every human being is uniquely loved by God. All are of equal value in his sight. Man made in God's image is endowed with a sufficient God-likeness to be able to enter into communion with him. He can find God's love constantly encountering him through people and situations and beauty, and is able to make a response of love. Many humanists too would assert that the meaning of life is love, but there is this difference. For them, the love is their own initiative. For the Christian, the love is a response to a greater which is there already.

The purpose is service. The Christian seeks to serve God with all his faculties, in all his motives, words, and actions. The mundane and trivial are included as well as the noble and spiritual. When all of life is seen as God's service, pleasures gain in richness and sorrow is borne with more stability. Life, instead of being a fragmented collection of joys and pains, fits together and begins to make sense.

Serving God is never, in the Christian view, to be set in opposition to the service of mankind. The one includes the other. A man 'cannot love God, whom he has not seen, if he does not love his brother, whom he has seen'.[2] Humanism has a high ideal of loving one's brother, and here it holds much common ground with Christianity. But Christians believe that the most effective and selfless service is given to mankind when it is seen as part of the service of God.

Christianity thus makes assertions which are totally opposed to the philosophy of meaninglessness. Moreover

[2] 1 John 4: 20. Unless otherwise indicated, biblical quotations in this chapter are from *Good News for Modern Man* (The New Testament in Today's English Version, Fontana Books).

the claim that 'God is, therefore life is meaningful' is no less consistent than the statement of the existentialist: 'God is dead, therefore life is meaningless.' It is also made on the basis of experience. If the existentialist could find himself believing, he would have a full cure for his predicament. Certainly there are many who have been kept from despair because even in desolation they were still able to believe in a God who loved them.

But there is another reason why Christians assert that human life has meaning. They believe that God himself entered human existence; not as a legend, handed down from generation to generation; not as a myth, as with the Greek stories of theophany; but as a fact of history, soberly recorded, whose date we can estimate to within three or four years, and in a town which we can visit today. Man is in God's image, but Christ is the Image of God.

In the man Jesus, Christians believe, God entered human existence, living it on the same terms as ourselves. In so doing he not only expressed in human terms what God is like (that is why he is called the Word, or expression of God), but also showed how a truly human life should be lived. Pilate, when Jesus was up for trial, exhibited him to the crowd and in derision cried out: 'Look! Here is the man.' Christians endorse that, but in a very different sense. Here they see true manhood; here in the strict sense is the normal man, the man to be followed. Though some of the details have been eroded away, it is still possible to know a great deal about his life from the records which were written down either by men who knew him or had intimate contact with those who did. The stories that have come down to us are quite sufficient to offer a very comprehensive pattern for human living.

From conventional standpoints it was a very ordinary life, just that of a small-town carpenter turned preacher in one of the least important outposts of the Roman

Empire. The conflicts which it raised were provincial and trivial. But when that life is examined more closely, it may be seen to have a stature which no other man has equalled, through its power, gentleness, boldness, tenderness, poise and self-giving. It is clear that Jesus lived out what he preached, a fact which his accusers could never deny. Although the Gospels show a life that has been called perfect, however, they do not portray a demigod. They portray a man.

If it really was the life of God on earth, as his followers came to believe when they pondered on its quality, it alters irrevocably our understanding of our own. This life shows the nature of God, not in abstract words or ethical precepts, but in concrete terms of human character, speech and action. A man is showing what God is like. A man is bearing unmarred the image of God. As we look at him perhaps we shall understand not only what is divine, but also what is human.

## The humanism of Christianity

Man was formed by God, and the purpose of his life is to serve his Creator. But how is he to do that? In the creation story we have already considered, a very interesting phrase is used which, though pre-scientific, is very much in accord with a modern understanding of personality. God makes man from dust, gives him life, and man becomes, as the older translations put it, 'a living soul'. This bears the meaning of a unity in which the various functions of man are intimately fused. 'Soul' is not here used in the Greek sense of a spirit distinct from a body; it means, rather, a single functioning unit in which what we term physical, mental and spiritual interpenetrate one another completely. This concept underlies the humanism of Christianity.

A pious Jew would have thought it inconceivable that farming or singing should be activities qualitatively different from prayer. All are expressions of the living soul. It would be meaningless to offer some of these activities to God and not them all. There is no true distinction between secular and sacred. Either the whole of life is offered to God, in which case the whole is sacred, or the whole is held back, in which case even 'religious' activities are not sacred at all.

The Bible therefore is the most earthy of all the great religious books. Even its spirituality is firmly grounded, with insistence on worship from the heart mentioned in the same breath as condemnation of sharp practice. The good life is certainly not seen as that of a contemplative mystic withdrawing himself from an evil world. Man, rather, seems to feel very much at home in the world, enjoying his part in the created order. He finds great satisfaction in the skill of the craftsman and the work of the artist. He loves music, both for pleasure and refreshment, and for praising God. He delights in the harvest and the seasons, in the power of nature and the curious ways of the wild animals. Probably the reverence and wonder that many European poets have felt about nature is a direct inheritance from the Jewish-Christian tradition, while appreciation of it is often lacking in cultures which have no clear belief in a Creator. The strength of the greatest nature poetry is that, beyond the splendour of the visible, it feels towards God revealing himself in beauty and wisdom.

The whole-hearted embracing of life as God's gift is clearly seen too in the biblical picture of marriage and family life. It is true that some of the early Christians, in their zeal for purity in an environment that knew very little sexual restraint, almost went so far as to deny that sexuality was God's gift at all. But in the Bible attraction, courtship, marriage and the delights of love physically expressed are all extolled. Like any gift they may be misused, but in themselves they are thoroughly good and to be thankfully received.

But in the biblical view man can never truly enjoy the world unless he enjoys it as a worshipper. He must gratefully acknowledge that all the richness of life is God's gift. He must see beyond the creation to the Creator. Prayer and worship must have their rightful place among all man's activities, for it may be that they are the most distinctively human thing about us.

Christians, therefore, like the humanists, can fairly claim that 'our concern is with this life'. But the Christian concern is different. Christians see themselves as guests in the universe, there to use responsibly and to enjoy what has been given. Humanists, rather, see themselves as hosts, to do with their existence what they will. And while humanists see life as bounded by the physical environment, Christians are always feeling beyond it. They are at home in the world, thoroughly at home. But no-one who has experienced God can feel that the world is his ultimate resting-place.

The religion which Jesus lived and taught endorses the life-affirmation of the Old Testament. He himself was a Jew and had breathed this tradition from childhood. His love of life can clearly be seen in the Gospels. His stories and illustrations frequently show his pleasure in the natural world. He was extremely sociable, to such an extent that his critics called him a glutton and a drinker. He certainly expressed his emotions: anger when he threw out the crooked businessmen in the Temple forecourt; grief when confronted with the death of a friend; fear as he anticipated the horror of crucifixion; compassion when he met with all forms of human need. It is possible still to detect his irony and humour despite the fact that his words have gone through two successive translations. The force of his personality, like that of Nietzsche's superman, was released creatively into life.

There is a common misunderstanding of Christianity at this point. Swinburne once wrote:

'Thou hast conquered, O pale Galilean;
the world has grown gray from thy breath.'

Somehow, contrary to all the evidence of the Gospels,
Jesus is made out to be a dreary figure, one who made
life insipid and robbed human pleasures of their
vitality. But the following of Jesus may be claimed to be
an enhancement of life because, while acknowledging a
secular humanism to the full, it never rests there. It adds
a spiritual dimension, and offers as reality that for which
the human spirit longs. This may be why some of the
greatest works of art, music and architecture have
turned out to be those with a Christian theme or
motive, and even in the twentieth century a number of
artists, though themselves not believers, have turned to
Christian subjects. It is also true that very little art of
merit has come from within the framework of an
explicit secularism, perhaps because there the spirit of
man is limited and tied.

But the teaching of Jesus is not a simple life-affirmation. It certainly has its stern and challenging aspect.
He was calling people to something beyond this world,
to the 'kingdom', to obedience and faith in God. And he
taught unequivocally that it was worth sacrificing
anything – riches, pleasures, prospects and even human
love – to enter that kingdom. He did not offer his
followers an easy time, for he spoke of self-sacrifice and
of 'taking up a cross', which in his day was the common
gallows and therefore a mark of shame. In other words,
his followers were to be prepared to be openly known as
such, even when it brought mockery and opposition.
The 'cross' meant unashamed committal, and sometimes following a road alone and misunderstood.
Christianity requires a man to stand by his convictions,
which is not always easy. It might even be necessary to
die for one's faith as Jesus himself did. Therefore if
Christianity is 'life-affirming' in one sense, it is 'life-

denying' in another, for it teaches that God must come first at all costs.

At this point the teaching of Jesus almost seems self-contradictory. The paradox is summed up in one of his most famous sayings, the only one to be recorded in all four Gospels: 'Whoever tries to save his own life will lose it; whoever loses his life will save it.'[3] He is teaching that the way to a truly rich experience of life is through self-forgetfulness, and being absorbed into a purpose bigger than ourselves. Self-interest often defeats its own end. The rich man is often miserable, the pampered bored and frustrated. Conversely, those who whole-heartedly give themselves up in concern for others are among the most joyful. Christianity teaches that the one in whom we are to lose our self-interest for ever is God. Then we find our life again, the same yet subtly transformed.

Humanists put humanity first. In the Christian view that ideal is disastrously incomplete, for it can easily become a sophisticated selfishness. Christians seek to put God first. This in no way lessens the call to be of service to humanity, but it puts that call into a different perspective, showing it to be part of something greater.

We have seen how Christianity has an ideal of personal self-expression, but directed God-wards. It must also be with discipline. Uncontrolled self-expression can be moral anarchy, as modern society knows all too well. There must be a direction, a channel, a structure. Christians believe the structure to be the law of God, a set of timeless principles given to man to live by, and within which to find his freedom. Seen in this way the Ten Commandments, far from being restrictions, are the very safeguards of liberty. Christianity here differs sharply from humanism, whose provisional moral codes often appear permissive and vague.

'Honour your father and mother' protects the in-

[3] Luke 17: 33.

tegrity of the family and communication between the generations. 'You shall not commit adultery' defines the right and wrong use of sex so that this immense drive may be expressed without reservation in a context of love and security. 'You shall not steal' enables community living. 'You shall not bear false witness' makes possible free and trusting human relationships. 'You shall not covet' paves the way for true contentment. 'You shall not' is not, as is sometimes imagined, the statement of an attitude to life; rather, it is a definition of the boundaries, so that within them there may be a fulfilment free from shame.

This can be seen in the first four Commandments also, which deal with man in relation to God. They ensure that man shall be a worshipper of the right God, in the right way. For whether a believer in God or not, man finds himself a worshipper. If he does not worship God, he will find some form of idolatry, to success or wealth or comfort, or even to himself. The first two Commandments therefore determine the object of worship, God alone. The third, not to take God's name in vain, deals with the nature of that worship, which must be sincere. The fourth, the sabbath law, ensures that there shall be time for it.

Jesus had a great deal to say about the law. His judgment was thoroughly to endorse its relevance, extending its scope beyond conduct to the realms of thought, motive and desire. The moralists of his day had defined and defined the details until the law had become a dead set of rules, obedience to which could lead only to self-righteousness. Jesus did exactly the opposite. He showed that the law was fundamentally concerned with man's attitude before his actions, so that outward conformity meant nothing without obedience from the heart.

Teaching about God's law or absolute moral standards often sounds strange to our modern age of expediency. It is often assumed that fulfilment can be found only in rejecting moral codes, though the evidence is often to the contrary. Certainly the experiments in moral lawlessness of the twentieth century have not been conspicuously successful even in bringing happiness. The Ten Commandments and the teaching of Jesus come from a culture very different from our own, which means that care and ingenuity may be needed in applying them to, say, trade union ethics or student revolt. But this is perfectly possible, though the Christian church has been slow to apply God's law to a changing world.

The humanism of Christianity, therefore, like that of the secularist, is an ideal of personal fulfilment and self-expression, of service to humanity. But Christians believe that these are only possible when man himself bows down to God and makes him the supreme end of his life.

## A moral failure

Modern existentialism, as we have seen, holds that man is in an acute state of isolation from his fellows. We are compelled to live close to others, but their presence is a source of irritation and anxiety, an intrusion and a threat. Sartre, in one of his plays, sums up the human predicament in the famous line, 'Hell is other people.'

This is clearly true to part of human experience, as anyone who has faced working with an incompatible colleague, suffered persecution on grounds of race or creed or, worse, lived through the failure of human love, can testify. The Christian faith here agrees with existentialism that this is a common state of affairs, but asserts that it need not always be so. Christianity sees man's alienation from his fellows as due to a deeper alienation. He is separated from God. Because God is the source of all being and self-giving, it is natural that those who are alienated from him should find it hard to make relationships with each other. In the Christian view, no radical solution to the conflict between man and man is to be found unless this deeper problem is solved. The existentialist simply has to accept the fact of alienation and live with it. The humanist often blandly ignores it. But Christianity claims both to give a correct diagnosis of the sickness of man's spirit and even to offer a cure by which men will be brought out of alienation from God and again into true relationship.

The Christian faith does not flatter at this point, for it asserts that mankind has deliberately turned away from God. Given an autonomy and some power of self-determination, he has wilfully abused it. Genesis speaks of man eating from the tree and being cast out of the garden; that is to say, he has taken upon himself the right to choose what is good and evil – by making himself into a god he has rejected the true God; he has broken the relationship and thwarted the purpose which God intended for him. Even the law of God, given as a guide for fruitful living, serves to catalogue the failure that has ensued.

Jesus once said this about the human heart: 'It is what comes out of a person that makes him unclean. For from the inside, from a man's heart, come the evil ideas which lead him to do immoral things, to rob, kill, commit adultery, covet, and do all sorts of evil things; deceit, indecency, jealousy, slander, pride, and folly – all these evil things come from inside a man and make him unclean.'[4] He is saying that the cause of our moral failure lies in the spring of our willing and desiring. We have turned from the right we do know; we have hidden from the little of God that we did understand. We have kept ourselves in a selfish comfort and security, refusing to have any master but ourselves, with the result that our actions are poisoned at their very source.

[4] Mark 7: 20–23.

The humanist will not admit this because in general he holds too hopeful a view of human nature, or regards a moral lapse as merely the unfortunate result of heredity and conditioning. Christianity, however, like existentialism, holds a clear doctrine of human responsibility. When the fullest allowance has been made for circumstances, men are still guilty of a deliberate turning from God and breach of his law. Christian values, though, are not the conventional ones. It may well be that in God's sight a religious man who is thoroughly self-righteous has rejected God much more completely than another whose conduct simply goes against the social taboos. The former stubbornly refuses to humble himself before God, while the other makes no pretence of goodness. Only God knows what allowances need to be made for individual cases. But judged according to the true scale of values, all mankind has failed and is guilty before him.

'There is not one who understands,
Or who seeks for God.
All men have turned away from God,
They have all gone wrong.
No one does what is good, not even one.'[5]

So wrote the apostle Paul. These words do appear at first sight to disparage so much that seems self-evidently good in human effort. But Paul is speaking of a divine judgment on the human heart which, until any individual is willing to admit is true about himself and even his own attempts at goodness, he will not find the way to restoration. Though no-one has the right to make that sort of judgment upon another, it is necessary for each, personally, to acknowledge his responsibility for selfishness and godlessness, his accountability to the Creator who is also his Judge.

[5] Romans 3: 11, 12 quoting Psalm 14.

Nietzsche and others claimed that this doctrine made men morally sick. Christianity, rather, suggests that it is only when men are realistic about their condition that they will wish to consult the doctor. But they should not then let their mind dwell on the illness. Having begun to apply the remedy, they will concentrate on health and vitality.

Deliberately so far I have not used the word 'sin' at all. Traditional theology and traditional religious language would put it thus: all human beings are born with the taint of original sin and go on sinning throughout their lives. This brings its inevitable consequence of spiritual death, which is separation from God. Original sin (though this is not meant to be an exhaustive definition) can be seen as the tragic fact that we are born into a world of alienated people. From birth and possibly before, the alienation of man from man is with us. First experienced in the fallibility of parental love, then in childhood quarrels, then in the gulf which separates the growing person from his parents, then perhaps in difficulties in marriage and, finally, in the loneliness of old age, this sense of alienation is with us, and as the existentialist writers so clearly understand, it goes as deep as anything we know of ourselves.

I have suggested that Christianity offers a way out of this predicament. The Christian church, when it is true to its own ideal, claims to be a group of human beings once alienated but now related to one another because they have come into a relationship with God. It is a plain fact, open to verification, that within a Christian group people of very different ages, colours, races, status, income and intelligence are able to co-exist in deep mutual understanding and harmony. Paul put it that in Christ 'there are no Gentiles and Jews, circumcised and uncircumcised, barbarians, savages, slaves, or free men, but Christ is all, Christ is in all'.[6] That list

[6] Colossians 3: 11.

contains some of the most mutually prejudiced groups that his world contained. It is a bold claim, but despite the manifest failure of parts of the institutional and visible church, anyone who has been within a genuine Christian fellowship knows that it is true.

How, then, is it possible for man to come again into relationship with God? By himself, man cannot do it. But God from his side has done it already. The clue to understanding this is to be found in what Christians believe to be the starkest expression of alienation ever to be uttered, Jesus' cry while he was dying on the cross: 'My God, my God, why did you abandon me?'[7] Here is a question springing from a terrible anguish, equal in quality to the darkest experiences of existentialism. It is almost a cry of 'God is dead'.

The words of theology are always approximations, and this is particularly true when we try to speak adequately about the spiritual dynamics of the cross. Christians believe that in the death of Jesus, God was bearing himself the alienation that has come into our world. He took upon himself the consequences of what we have done. Like anyone who has been wronged and seeks a reconciliation, he bears the pain and loss himself. God took the alienation fully upon himself, going to its very depths and exhausting it. In so doing he abolished it and made a way of peace for any who would accept what he has done.

All this has great relevance to the problem of guilt, with which perhaps Kafka was dealing in *The Trial*. Christianity says unequivocally that all are guilty before God. But we must make a clear distinction between guilt-feelings and actual guilt. There are certain actions, the transgressions of a social code more than of divine law, which can be highly charged with guilt-feelings, while some evident inhumanity may have no association of guilt at all. For example, someone might

[7] Matthew 27: 46.

feel very guilty about not going to church twice on Sunday and perfectly at ease about his neglect of his children. The first step in the Christian healing of guilt is to attribute it rightly, to distinguish between scruple and disobedience. Then Christianity offers a full forgiveness for the actual guilt because in Jesus God has taken the consequences of it upon himself.

Those who receive pardon for their true failures, and really accept that they are forgiven, can then find release from their irrational feelings of guilt. The objective removal of guilt, Christians believe, is instantaneous; but the deliverance from guilty feelings – the cleansing of the conscience – may take time. You are accepted by God, says Tillich; now 'accept that you are accepted'. That is why the Christian religion speaks of salvation by grace, which means that God in his kindness gives to man what is beyond his power to work for or achieve; forgiveness, reconciliation, the restoration of the relationship which has been lost.

But every individual who wants it must receive it personally. God does not deal with humanity in the mass, but with individuals. Therefore I must accept my own responsibility for my own failure; whatever help and guidance I have received from other human beings, I must come alone to God and cast myself upon his mercy. Although this will be the most solitary thing I ever do, it brings me into company, possibly the first real company I have known.

## The overcoming man

The idea of grace, of a loving initiative from beyond man, has no counterpart in humanism or existentialism. We have seen how Christians believe that the reconciliation between God and man is an act of grace from God's side. But more than that; in grace God not only does for man what he does not deserve, but makes him what he could not otherwise be. Against philosophies of man making himself, Christianity speaks of God working within, making new persons, giving life in a new mode. No amount of religion or self-improvement, no accumulation of good deeds can achieve this. It is something which comes from God, to which man can only respond. The Christian ideal of the overcoming man, to borrow Nietzsche's phrase for the man who has gained mastery over life and self, is of one made new by grace.

There is a strange interview recorded in the Fourth Gospel, in which an eminent teacher of religion, a good and fair-minded man named Nicodemus, comes to Jesus one night to question him. While Nicodemus is still on his preliminaries Jesus seems to cut him short, comes straight to the point, and tells him that he must be 'born again'. Even to a highly-trained Jewish theologian those words have an unfamiliar ring. Nicodemus is puzzled. 'How can a grown man be born again? . . . He certainly cannot enter his mother's womb and be born a second time!'[8]

Jesus is using a metaphor. He is describing a change, or renewal, so total that it can best be pictured in this way. Among all the biblical illustrations of this change, the second birth is the most graphic. There can be no question that here is the heart of the New Testament message: the claim that God in his grace bestows a new order of life to those who will humbly accept his gift. Sometimes false emphasis in the teaching of the church or popular misunderstandings have obscured the teaching of the New Testament and reduced the Christian religion to a moral struggle or a following of the example of Jesus with the help of prayer. But anything less than the offer of restoration and re-creation is sub-Christianity. Christianity purports to be good news before it is an ethical code.

[8] John 3: 4.

The new birth occurs at the point where a human being, knowing his failure and inadequacy, comes to God for forgiveness and life, and offers himself to God's re-creative power.

For some the new birth is traumatic, accompanied by great inner conflicts and agonies. Paul's was like this. Conversion for him meant a total re-orientation of his values. He had, in effect, to come to the point of admitting that his effort was utterly misdirected, and his way of life unhappiness and folly. For a man openly committed to the persecution of Christianity this was no easy thing to do. The result of his inner struggle was so devastating that it involved a temporary collapse of his very forceful ego, after which he went away alone for a period to think out the implications of what had happened to him, and was another ten years before he set out on his intensely active work as a missionary. The new birth cannot but be traumatic for those whose attitude has hardened in ways that are un-Christian. To deny what one has accepted for half a lifetime, and to affirm what one has laughed at or denied, is painful and costly. The subsequent adjustments may take years.

For others the new birth is so quiet and unobtrusive that it is hardly noticed at the time, although the results that gradually follow are momentous. This is often the case for those who come from Christian homes and feel that faith has been theirs since childhood, or for some who become Christians in adolescence, before their personalities have set in some definite mould. There are many Christians who can put no date or time to the new birth, but are in no doubt that it has happened.

When a person has been born again the signs become clearly discernible: a hunger for spiritual nourishment; an understanding of Christian language as if it had become real and three-dimensional; an assurance of being reconciled with God; an inner sense that Christ is a living person. Just as many an existentialist has said

113

from his experience 'God is dead – for me', so the born again may say: 'God is very much alive and real – for me'.

The new life grows through months and years. There will be many falls and discouragements, as much as any child finds when it tries to crawl, walk, run, swim. There will almost certainly be one-sided growth at some stage – an immature enthusiasm or a claim to too much knowledge – just as with any growing person. Sometimes there will be revolt, like that of an adolescent who has to do so to test his convictions and establish his own identity. Almost certainly doubt and questioning will come, for that is the means of deeper understanding. The growth to maturity is gradual. But in spiritual life there is no growing old. When the body becomes fragile and exhausted, and even the mind loses its clarity, spiritual vitality and growth may continue.

At this point the Christian religion is empirically verifiable. Anyone who has been able to observe a church or movement which keeps to the Christianity of the Bible can see for himself the changes made in individual lives, and the difference between the unbeliever and the Christian in extreme old age, when most of the comforts and hopes of life have gone.

The new birth does not mean that a person's fundamental endowment of temperament or individual psychology is altered. Those things are the raw material of our existence. Christians may suffer as much as any others from the illnesses of body or mind, or from the stresses that can come to a sensitive personality. Christianity is no insurance policy against the vicissitudes of life. But the new birth does mean that the character is gradually changed, for character is what the raw material becomes as it is influenced. The dishonest becomes truthful; the idle, hardworking; the fearful, bold; the sullen, sweet-tempered; the shiftless, reliable; the selfish, concerned for others. This is a slow process, and it is never complete in this life. God does not go about his new creation in a hurry, any more than he did the first. But he does recreate from within, until the qualities of the life of Christ, love, joy, peace, patience, kindness, goodness, faithfulness, humility, self-control, are produced as spontaneously as fruit by a tree. Paul lists these virtues as being produced by the Spirit,[9] meaning by the natural outworking of a life in which the Spirit of God dwells; that is, a life made new.

I have suggested that the new birth does not alter temperament. A better use, however, can be made of it. If Christ gives self-control, we are less at the mercy of our natural waywardness. If Christ brings joy and peace, we are less vulnerable to our natural moods and discontents. Perhaps, too, the restoration of a relationship with God means a greater measure of self-acceptance and self-forgiveness, which are most necessary for inner peace.

The New Testament frequently uses the phrase 'eternal life' as another way of speaking of that dimension of life which a person enters when he is born again. Translations are incorrect when they render the phrase as 'everlasting life', implying simply a long duration in time. Rather, it means life that belongs to a dimension beyond this world. Perhaps men came to believe in its everlastingness because of what they had experienced of its quality – rather like the feeling of lovers that their love is of such a nature that it can have no end. Certainly there was a time when the Jews had only a very dim concept of life after death, but a burning sense of the reality of God in the present.

So eternal life in the New Testament sense begins here and now. But it is of such an order that it goes on beyond death. The life after death as Christians believe in it is not a shadowy reflection of this present life, a kind of dismal Hades. If anything, it is the exact

[9] Galatians 5: 22, 23.

opposite. This life is the shadow, the threshold, the incomplete, while the life to come is the full-blooded, the solid, the real.

C. S. Lewis fancifully pursued this idea in *The Great Divorce*. A bus-load of the occupants of hell are taken on a visit to heaven, and may stay there if they wish. The visitors find that by heaven's standards they are insubstantial – they barely exist at all. Heaven is immensely solid: the raindrops weigh tons; the blades of grass are strong as steel. The more in accord with the spirit of heaven the visitors are, the more substantial they too become, but those who cannot face its ways fade away to nothing.

This is why Christians affirm in the Creed, 'I believe in the resurrection of the body', not 'I believe in the immortality of the soul'. The body of course does not mean the atoms and molecules of which we are at present composed. They are only borrowed from a general pool and we return them within a very few years anyway. It means the real us, the whole us. Beyond this affirmation, Christians may not claim a fuller knowledge. The heightened language of the end of the book of Revelation is not giving a description of the geography and furnishings of heaven. It is teaching that heaven is the ultimate best, the supreme bliss, the satisfying of all desire and yearning, the meeting with God face to face and the worship of him eternally.

All this is implied in the doctrine of the new birth. Although it is a profoundly other-worldly doctrine, it is not, as some detractors of Christianity say, a sort of insurance policy; a basic premium paid now in the form of unwelcome duty and discipline to attain a considerable endowment hereafter. The evidence is very strong that far from incapacitating people for the present, a Christian faith brings new motivation and hope, a zest for living, and stability and resilience for those who suffer.

Moreover, no-one can be genuinely a Christian without feeling what Douglas Steere has called 'unlimited liability for one another'. A glance at world history in the last few hundred years will show that many of the major breakthroughs of science, and almost all the serious attempts to spread medicine and education to those without them, have been made by Christians. Indeed, it may be argued against the humanist view of history as the gradual conquest of superstition by reason that the development of science and the widespread practical application of human compassion could occur only within a culture that believed in a loving and rational God. Christianity when practised in the manner of its founder is neither escapist nor futuristic. The founder himself spent the greater part of his public work in deeds of kindness, and the greater part of his teaching was about a style of life in which love was the driving force. He did, however, constantly give warning that those who view this present life in material and intellectual terms only are blind and foolish.

The overcoming man, as the Christian sees him, is the man who has been reconciled with God, has received new life, and is being inwardly transformed. Not in his own strength, but by the grace of God, he is able gradually to master himself, is given power to live and love and finally to face death with confidence.

## Immersed in suffering

The humanists' approach to suffering is simple. They feel bound to remove it where possible, with all the energy they can muster and with all the means at their disposal. As we have already seen, men and women of essentially humanist conviction are to be found at work in all humanitarian causes: the relief of famine, medical practice and research, and education – frequently with an altruism that appears to transcend the pedestrian tenets of their creed. The fact of suffering presents no intellectual problem; there is only the pragmatic one of what to do about it.

The existentialist position is very different. Suffering, despair, anguish are simply part of the meaninglessness within which man has to live, and if possible live courageously. Again there is no intellectual problem, merely the practical one of living as a sufferer and mastering despair. If existentialists are less involved than humanists in the relief of suffering, this is the direct consequence of the extreme individualism of their approach to life.

But the Christian cannot look at suffering in quite so simple a way. Suffering is a mystery, if by that we mean a problem in which we are personally involved, and through which, though we do not understand it fully, we can gain a deeper insight into our existence. Suffering, like love and joy, is too profound for mere rationalistic discussion. We can never stand back from it as if it were a problem in mathematics.

Intellectually, of course, there is the question of how to reconcile belief in a good, almighty God with so much in the world that seems to be destructive, wasteful and meaningless. It is only for those who believe in a good God that such a question arises at all. This is not a new problem, however, discovered, as is sometimes implied, by the agnostics of the last 100 years. All the time man was coming to believe in a good God, he was suffering too. Chronologically, it is probably true to say that the experience of suffering preceded the formulation of any doctrine about God, and that belief in a good God has come about in the face of pain.

At the level of experience, therefore, it seems that men can both suffer and believe in God. But although Christianity can go some way to meeting the intellectual question, it cannot offer a complete solution. We will first see what it does have to say about the problem of suffering and then later become more practical.

Consider a few examples of suffering: thousands killed or made homeless by an earthquake; starvation and death to innocent people as a result of war; the loneliness and anxiety of old age; the anguish of depression and other mental illness; the birth of deformed or idiot babies due to unforeseen complications from a drug; the breaking up of a marriage; the encroachment of a slow and fatal illness. In some of these, possibly the majority, human selfishness, weakness or negligence are involved. A great deal of suffering has been brought by man himself, and therefore man is to blame for it. But there is also much for which there is no human cause at all.

Suffering can be one of the most creative of all experiences, if faced with humility and fortitude. Indeed, would it be possible for the greatest human qualities to be aroused and exercised without it? The greatest heroism may be found in a patient enduring a long and painful illness; the greatest devotion and care may be shown in the family with a deformed or retarded child; the greatest patience by those who deal with an imbecile; the greatest long-suffering by the persecuted. Adversity does not always arouse these qualities but often it does, and in the most unlikely people. Certainly, if human existence were made up of day after day of comfort and pleasure, if our life really was what the humanists sometimes appear to want to make it, there would be no scope for our highest and our best. Thus sometimes it is only through the facing of disaster and anguish that we come to know our true humanity.

To say this sort of thing is dangerously near callousness, for it appears almost to welcome suffering, and it is much more easily said by someone in good health and spirits than by one who suffers. But Christians are never asked to welcome suffering. They are always committed to the utmost activity in the relief of it, as Jesus himself was. They will never treat calamity with resignation as something God has sent. But where suffering is inescapable or irremediable they seem to have resources to face it and even to use it creatively, accepting it as something God has permitted. Jesus shrank from the prospect of the cross but, convinced that there was no other way, went through with it in peace.

These two points, that suffering is often caused by human failure and the fact that suffering can evoke man's best, alleviate the intellectual problem but do not solve it. There remains much that appears to be simply destructive. Why does a good God allow that? It is here that we come face to face with the mystery.

In the Bible this question is very powerfully and dramatically treated in the book of Job. Job is a good man, yet he has to suffer. We meet him first in the height of his prosperity and happiness when, suddenly, his comfortable existence is shattered. His flocks are stolen; his possessions are destroyed; his nearest and dearest are killed in a tornado; then Job himself is afflicted with a disfiguring and painful disease. Thus, poignantly, the question is posed. Why does God allow even the innocent to suffer? Is he in control and is he just?

Job's friends come and offer advice – it can hardly be called sympathy – based on the assumption that his suffering is the result of his wrongdoing and that he should mend his ways. But Job, though he knows his imperfections, also knows that he is not disproportionately worse than his friends. Feeling that the justice of the universe has been violated, that life is meaningless, he enters the darkest experiences of doubt, anguish and near-total disillusionment, a despair that is almost suicidal.

But gradually he comes to see further. His soul reaches out towards belief in immortality; perhaps the final justice is beyond this life. He comes to believe in a deeper way that God is still mighty and just, and it ill behoves man to argue with him. Then at last Job finds satisfaction. God speaks to him from a whirlwind, reminding him that he is a mere man who has no right to question the ways of the Almighty. He points Job to the many questions that man cannot answer, the wonder of creation in the earth, the sea, the snow, the storm, the stars. He reminds him of the power and freedom of the wild animals, and such apparent absurdities of nature as the ostrich, the hippopotamus and the crocodile. In a roundabout way God is telling him that the true scheme of things is much grander than is encompassed by Job's little philosophy. So Job is humbled and he acknowledges: 'I know you can do all things, and no purpose of yours can be thwarted. . . . I had heard of you from others, but now I see you myself. . . . Therefore I repent from the bottom of my heart.'[1]

Thus Job sees himself as he truly is, and understands something of God as he is. After this moment of truth his prosperity is restored. The point of the story surely is this: not that Job regained his riches and security, but that in the encounter with God he found the answer for which he was looking. His intellectual problem about the cause of his suffering was never rewarded with a solution. There was no solution, but there was an answer; God himself, whom Job had to learn to trust in the darkness. This met his need at a much deeper level than that of mind. It met his emotions and will and loyalty, the point where suffering had occurred.

It would be possible to deride all this by saying that it simply sidesteps a major obstacle to belief in God by placing the answer beyond the mind. But that is too superficial. It is a plain fact of experience that, though suffering is intellectually inexplicable, it is often the dimension in which faith becomes really faith and men

[1] Job 42: 2–6 (a loose paraphrase).

come to maturity. And those who trust God are frequently able to face great suffering without bitterness, with patience and even humour. Christians, too, have always been known to die courageously, as bear witness a succession of heroic men and women from the martyrs thrown to the lions in the first century to the many who have lost their lives for their faith in Africa in the last 100 years. Confronted with suffering, it is really the humanist view that seems inadequate because it scarcely reckons with the mystery of it; confronted with a sufferer, it may well be the humanist who has nothing to say.

The Christian faith adds an important insight to the message of the book of Job, which leaves us with a mystery and an almighty God. The Christian religion asserts that God himself is involved in the suffering of his creation. In the person of Jesus, God entered human life on the same terms as ourselves, including the experience of suffering. It is well known that how much a person suffers depends on his sensitivity. May we not suppose then that, as the supreme man, he knew the fullest pain? Insult and rejection would give him greater sorrow; being flogged and nailed to a cross would hurt him more. In his darkest hour, he cries out as if God has abandoned him; he, too, feels the desolation and meaninglessness of the abyss. Only, he feels it with an intensity granted to no other man.

If it is true that in Jesus God was suffering, there is comfort and reassurance. Whatever we may go through, however dark and inexplicable, God knows and understands, through experience; in a sense he goes through it with us too.

'I am poorly paid, I am unemployed, I live in a
    slum, I have tuberculosis. . . .
I am cold, God says, I am hungry, I am naked,
I am imprisoned, laughed at, humiliated . . .

I moan, riddled with shrapnel; I collapse under
 the volley of machine-gun fire,
I sweat men's blood on all battlefields,
I cry out in the night and die in the solitude of
 battle.'[2]

Christians, then, first see suffering as an evil to be
overcome. They are followers of one who took great
trouble with the sick, the insane, the hungry, the
anxious, the rejected. Christians have been and always
will be committed to the same work. Their effective-
ness at it is beyond question, as many a hospital, hostel
or refuge for social outcasts will bear witness. There is,
in fact, a Christian way of caring which, because it is
sensitive to the mystery of suffering, may bring a greater
comfort than the easy answers of secularism could ever do.

But, for the Christian, suffering can never simply be
an evil to overcome, nor can it simply be a way in
which life's meaninglessness confronts us. Like the existentialists, Christians see suffering as something in-
escapably bound up with our existence. It is, paradoxically, one of the things that makes us human. Anyone
who has been through acute suffering knows how it
strips away all superficial covering and exposes the core
beneath. But, if the core is exposed, it need not be
exposed for destruction; rather it may be exposed to the
love of God.

John, in his Gospel, has a curious habit of referring to
the suffering of Jesus as his 'glory'. To John the most
glorious moment does not seem to be the resurrection
morning, but the lifting up of Jesus on the cross. And so
Christians cannot only see suffering as a problem to be
dealt with; certainly they do not seek to revel in it
masochistically. But when unavoidable suffering does
come they seek to use it creatively. In John's sense, they
use it gloriously.

[2] M. Quoist, *Prayers of Life* (Gill).

## The Christian way of knowing

In the first part of this book we saw how the humanist position is based fundamentally on reason, to such an extent that humanists themselves now admit that they make an act of faith in it. Then we saw how the existentialists, in believing that this life has no meaning or rationality, repudiate the idea of objective knowledge and deny reason any ultimate validity. Each is setting out a way of 'knowing'; the first by reason and the second by intuition or arbitrary choice. What is the Christian way of knowing? On what sort of ground does a Christian hold beliefs such as those we have just considered?

The Christian way of knowing is through the combined exercise of reason and faith. Both are necessary for a mature Christian outlook, one that is genuinely faith and not a form of rationalism overlaid with piety, but yet which at the same time is not mere subjectivism, at the mercy of changing moods and fancies. First, then, we must look at the rational case for Christianity and see how far this takes us. Although this in itself is a subject for one book or several, an outline will be given here to show at least the sources from which the evidence comes.

A few hundred years ago, and in some quarters even until recently, much was made of the 'proofs for the existence of God'. It was claimed that by a process similar to Euclidean geometry the existence of God could be deduced from the natural world. Influenced as we are today by linguistic analysis, we would certainly no longer speak of 'proofs' in the sense of logical steps leading to the conclusion that God is. Proofs of this sort need axioms, and no statement could be more axiomatic, more supra-logical, than 'God is'. This could never be deduced.

The 'proofs' for God's existence really stand as a

witness that in all lands and cultures there are men who find themselves believers in God and, finding themselves so, have used their rational faculty to try to prove what they already believe. The 'proofs' or arguments for God are in methodology more like those of natural science: inductive, seeking to provide explanations that fit the facts. And as such they still have some validity.

The ontological 'proof' sought to argue from the presence of the idea of God in the mind to the existence of God himself. Although such a step is logically impossible, the fact remains that almost all peoples do have a concept of the Deity. At least one explanation is that God has implanted the idea of himself into men's minds that they might search for him. This is no bolder an explanation than that of the psychologist who suggests that it is all wish-fulfilment.

The 'proof' from design was an attempt to argue from the order and pattern in the universe to the existence of a designer. It is logically not possible to prove it, but this is at least one explanation of the beautiful complexity of the world as revealed by science. Even the adaptation of living forms to their environment, which is sometimes presented as a process of blind chance, can be seen as part of God's technique.

Another 'proof' of God was based on the moral sense, the feeling of duty, of obligation, of 'ought', that all or most men possess, which goes far beyond the dictates of prudence or reason. One explanation of the presence of the moral faculty is that it was implanted by a moral God. The psychologists are fond of discovering the origins of morality in the relationship of the infant with its parents. This is perfectly acceptable to the Christian who simply holds that, in so far as theory is correct, it has described the way God works.

This brief account of the arguments for God is totally undeveloped but perhaps shows the sort of way in which they are relevant. The induction that 'God is' is for each argument at least a possibility. Of course there is nothing specifically Christian in these arguments, which could apply to any theistic religion.

But Christianity makes a distinct historical claim, by which it stands or falls. It is that God entered human life within recorded history, and that there is a reliable record in the New Testament both of what happened and of its impact on the men who thus met with God on earth. The New Testament has been subjected to the most searching and sceptical scrutiny during the last 100 years, to which it has stood up very well. The abundance of manuscripts and the early date of some means that there can be little doubt about what the authors actually wrote. Those parts of the New Testament which can be verified by archaeological remains and the secular writings of contemporary historians, strongly support the substantial historicity of its background. I say 'background' deliberately, because there is very little about the central events of the Christian gospel to be found in early documents outside the New Testament.[3] (And why should there be, considering that Christianity for its first fifty years was generally thought of as a mere sect within the despised Jewish faith?) But we do know a good deal about the leading characters and places of the time: Pilate, Caiaphas, Herod the Great, Gallio, Jerusalem, Antioch, Corinth. The New Testament is verifiably accurate over these, Luke especially having been shown to be a thoroughly reliable historian. If so, it is reasonable to claim a similar degree of accuracy for the biblical account of the birth, life, death and resurrection of Jesus. Certainly it is prejudice, not reason, that dismisses this as impossible.

Suppose, then, that the Gospels and Acts are at least a fair record of events as judged by the standard of the historical writing of the day. Then we must provide an

[3] See Michael Green, *Runaway World* (Inter-Varsity Press) for a survey of such evidence as there is.

explanation of the person of Jesus as portrayed there. We must account for the absolutely central claim about his resurrection, which it seems was never effectively controverted at the time, and then the rapid spread of this faith all over the then civilized world. One very reasonable explanation of all this is simply that Jesus was God and Christianity is true.

There is another source of evidence for the truth of Christianity which we may term pragmatic, the evidence of faith at work. I have several times made statements about the effects of Christianity, suggesting that they are empirically verifiable: the unity and brotherhood that Christians can experience; the transformation of character which occurs through conversion; the radiance of the elderly who have Christian faith in contrast to those who do not; the capacity of Christians for compassion and self-sacrifice; the courage with which they generally face suffering and death. If these claims are correct, here again is a strong argument for belief. If Christianity works, it may well be true.

None of these evidences, inductive, historical, pragmatic, is in itself sufficient to compel assent. None of them is complete by itself. But they do all converge; it is this, rather than any single argument in isolation, that forms the intellectual case for the truth of Christianity.

Thus reason may take a man part way to Christian conviction, but by itself it can never make him a Christian. At some point faith and commitment must take over. Existential Christians have sometimes likened faith to a leap in the dark, an idea which can be dangerously misunderstood. It does not mean simply leaping out in a desperate hope that there might be something there. It is not a plunge across an utterly dark abyss. Of course a leap must be made, but it is made from reasonable ground. Faith is, rather, the considered commitment of a thoughtful person using all his faculties. Though it goes beyond reason, it does not violate it. And when Augustine wrote, 'I believe in order that I may understand', he implied that anyone who has made the step of faith has entered a wider field for the use of his reason.

Now it was at this point that Kierkegaard parted company with the general Christian tradition which followed Augustine in laying emphasis on both reason and faith. Because Kierkegaard found that the Christianity of his time had become largely a matter of 'man's wisdom', in his extreme reaction he emphasized faith so much that reason was neglected or even positively denied. He went so far as to say that Christianity is absurd, but yet must be believed. Kierkegaard's religion requires a continual crucifixion of the intellect. This means that the believer, never being convinced in his mind, cannot give the full assent of his personality to God. He cannot believe with integrity. This is a serious departure from the Christianity of Christ who, though proclaiming what purported to be a revelation of God's truth, constantly appealed to the mind and critical faculty.

On the other hand, some theologians have gone so far in their emphasis on reason that real faith has become unnecessary. There have been various attempts in Christian history to create complete theological systems, the two most famous being the *Summa* of Thomas Aquinas, which is still the corner-stone of Roman Catholic theology, and the *Institutes of the Christian Religion* by John Calvin. Both these thinkers were far too wise and subtle to forget about faith. But at times the result of their systematization has been to diminish the necessity for it. If every problem that concerns you deeply has a neat answer, completely tied up, which can be found on a certain page of a theological encyclopaedia, where is the need for faith? Christianity so treated always runs the danger of becoming just another glib rationalistic system, only with God as the key idea;

as inadequate for the deep needs of humanity as rational humanism itself.

A Christian reared in this sort of religion once asked me: 'I used to know the answer to the problem of evil, but now I have forgotten it. Could you please remind me?' It was against the devastating shallowness of this sort of attitude that Kierkegaard revolted. There can be neither lasting security nor satisfaction within an enclosed system of thought. God's truth is far larger than any man-made theological framework. A number of times in history it appears that God has set aside the accepted theology and made some new truth known outside it. He refuses, it seems, to be contained within our systems.

Earlier we thought of faith as a leap. Now we must change the metaphor to something more personal. Faith is trusting. Faith in a human being implies a trust, a willingness to leave one's interest in his hands, a committal. Christian faith is a personal committal to Christ. Like human trust it is something which goes far beyond reason and, like human trust, it is the entry into a realm of rich experience and personal knowledge that transcends the logical. In Christian understanding, committal to Christ is the entry into eternal life; it is the beginning of that personal knowledge whereby Jesus becomes a friend, not an idea, and the sense of forgiveness not a theory but a fact.

So Christianity differs from both humanism and existentialism in its way of knowing. It does not, like extreme existentialism, deny the validity of reason; nor, like humanism, does it give it first place. It claims not to violate reason, but to go beyond it. The Christian's deepest knowledge is reached through an act of faith that is completely personal. In this sense Christian truth is existential.

Let us now compare the three views of man on two of the most fundamental issues – human life itself, and man's role in it.

First, what value and what prospect does each give to human existence? Humanism traditionally has held a very optimistic view. Almost until the present day, belief was held, if not in the perfectibility of man, at least in his unlimited capacity for progress and his almost unbounded power to grow in goodness. To be a humanist even of a more cautious sort one must believe that life is thoroughly worth while even if it does not go on for ever.

The optimism of humanism is commendable, but must be criticized as unrealistic because it takes no proper account of man's moral failure, and certainly has no remedy to offer. There is nothing comparable to 'you must be born again', no renewal, no forgiveness. All humanism can offer is the hope of self-betterment for mild cases of failure, and perhaps psychiatry for those whose moral lapse represents a serious departure from normality. Humanism proposes a noble ethic, but it offers neither restoration nor power. It may be a creed for those who by normal standards are upright and self-sufficient, but it has nothing to say to those who have failed. Its near-total silence on the subject of guilt, suffering, despair and death means that it is irrelevant where man's personal need is most acute.

Man is incurably religious, as some humanists admit.

This part of his nature, concerned with his innermost fears and aspirations, must find fulfilment. But it is hard to see how what Sir Julian Huxley called 'experiences of transcendent rapture' could ever be conveyed through the mediation of the Secular Societies. Humanist suggestions about a religion of their own always seem slightly ludicrous and artificial, on a level with the Arch-Community-Songster of Canterbury in *Brave New World*. Humanist optimism, therefore, is too superficial to do justice to our humanity.

Atheistic existentialism, by contrast, sees life in much more sombre colours. Its great force and its enduring appeal is that it does seem relevant to life as we live it. The novels and plays of existentialism contain many telling portrayals of man's bewilderment and the failure of human relationships, all of which experience verifies. No doubt some of the extremes in modern literature have been produced for sensationalism, or titillation of gullible audiences. But it would be a mistake to dismiss it all as that. The continued presence of the theatre of violence and the absurd surely indicates that the message rings true.

But this sort of picture of man is not the whole truth; there is also evidence to be found in the rich moments of life. From these we know that human beings can have friendship, can love, can find a meaning in their existence, can live and die in hope. Because existentialism frequently denies these experiences it repels us as insufficient for a total philosophy of life. If humanism involves an unwarranted act of faith, existentialism appears to involve an unwarranted act of despair.

Christianity is neither so naïvely hopeful as the one, nor so pessimistic as the other. Like existentialism, it begins with man in his fear and isolation, but it insists that this, far from being the truly human state, is due to a breach with God into which we were born and which we perpetuate by our own wills. According to Christianity, there is a way back into meaning and purpose. The conditions are plain: an act of the will in turning from known wrongdoing; the receiving of God's forgiveness as something given by his generosity totally beyond our deserts; and a life of obedience to his will as far as it is known.

Making this claim Christianity can fairly offer itself as a religion for every sort of person: those who are naturally honest and respectable by human standards, and those who are not. Perhaps it is especially for those who know they are not, for it was the avowed aim of Jesus 'not to call the respectable people, but the outcasts', and he succeeded. The Christian church, carrying on what he began, has manifestly succeeded also, as anyone may check by finding out what a variety of people make up a living Christian congregation.

The second issue on which we must make comparison is man's role in life. What should he be doing in the world? The appeal of humanism is that it has a ready-made programme for action; it has definite targets at which to aim. Humanism is looking for a free society and for world peace, freedom from hunger, disease and oppression. It has an objective for the individual too, in terms of his health, security, happiness and self-fulfilment. Through kindness and insight the human race is to go forward.

But here humanism comes against its major stumbling-block. It is almost powerless to achieve these things. To make generalizations about society and what men ought to do is easy; to get them to do it is far harder. Humanism cannot transform the individual. 'It may take a generation', wrote Julian Huxley in 1943 of the principles of evolutionary ethics as he then conceived them, 'to translate these arid-sounding generalities into concrete terms and satisfying forms.' A generation has elapsed since he said that. Now we have entered what in many ways is a more violent age, the age of the bomb and the 'bomb culture' and all that it entails. If anything is to be a moral force in the world as we know it, it must have a great deal more thrust behind it than the arid generalities of humanism, whose efforts, though well-meaning, are puny in comparison with the task.

Existentialism, on the other hand, offers no general programme for social action, no scheme for bettering the human lot. There can be no sincere joining of a cause or a movement because it is not really possible to work for the good of others. Man by himself must work out his way of life, at the deepest level cut off from his fellows and in competition with them.

Now it would be easy simply to dismiss existentialism as a philosophy for the selfish and inconsiderate, but this would miss the point. Existentialism is trying to tell us that altruism is actually impossible. Therefore it is more honest, though less respectable, to pursue a policy of unashamed self-interest. A true existentialist could not run a business as a co-operative enterprise; rather, it would be for his pocket or his prestige. He could not join a trade union to further the interest and solidarity of the group; it would be for personal security alone. He could not be married for love of another, for the joy of sharing and giving; it could only be for stability, comfort or gratification. To those who attribute to themselves more idealistic motives the existentialist might retort: 'I am the only honest man among you. We are selfish, every one of us, but I at least admit it.'

At this point humanism and existentialism are almost diametrically opposed. But they are united in rejecting any concept of life beyond this present measurable one. Christianity, however, claims that life is more. There is an eternal dimension, to be known even in the present, breaking into everyday life at any moment, through a sunset or a bird's song, an act of kindness, an honest apology, an experience of love, an answered prayer, a passage from the Bible suddenly filled with meaning.

Life itself demands that we make a response to God.

I believe that any philosophy which reckons only with our finitude does not do justice to what we know of life. It does not measure up to the deeper experiences of the human spirit, not only love and joy but also anguish and desolation. Ernest Gordon, describing how human values were rediscovered by a disintegrating community in a Japanese prison-camp through a turning to Christianity,[4] aptly quotes Dostoievsky: 'The one essential condition of human existence is that man should always be able to bow down before something infinitely great. If men are deprived of the infinitely great they will not go on living and die of despair.' Thus, I believe, both humanism and existentialism deny what is an essential part of our human nature, our aspiration to God. It could indeed be argued that this is the very thing which makes us human. A way of life which denies it can never command man's deep allegiance or respect.

This does not in any way mean that Christianity is not concerned for our present existence. Christianity thoroughly endorses the humanist social programme; indeed it can fairly claim to have invented most of it. And it is quite clear that despite their failures Christians are and always have been in the forefront of all ventures to advance medicine, education, science and agriculture, and all works of practical compassion. Christianity simply asserts that though this life is important, it is not everything. 'Man cannot live on bread alone.'[5]

I believe that man without God is inadequate to face all that life may bring. He cannot deal with personal tragedy and darkness in the most creative way. He lacks the inner rest and motive power even to be of the greatest use in the world. The Christian religion begins by saying that man's first duty is to love God with heart, mind and

[4] E. Gordon, *Miracle on the River Kwai* (Collins). A profoundly human book.

[5] Matthew 4: 4.

134

strength. It then goes on to give him a task in the world, to love his neighbour as himself. Humanists seek to improve the conditions of our life; the sincerity with which they go about it is unquestionable, and their efficiency often puts Christians to shame. But Christianity starts by renewal of the man in bringing him to God, and so seeks to better the world.

Christians do not have Utopian expectations, but their creed has many times proved to be the force that renewed degenerate society. Moreover, the Christian religion has often found new channels of expression when the existing ones were obsolete. There are signs that this is occurring today. While the institutional church and many of its structures seem dead or dying, an informal Christianity, surprisingly like that of the New Testament, is very much alive. Perhaps it is this faith, expressed in a contemporary way, that alone can bring order from our present moral chaos.

For these reasons I believe that Christianity is a more human way than humanism. Humanists may claim an ancient tradition for their way of thinking, but their movement even in its most modern dress bears still the marks of its Victorian ancestry, when Christian belief often seemed unacceptable although the Christian ethic was desired. Many of the values of the Victorian age were Christian in their origin. Even Thomas Huxley in his private melancholy sang hymns with his agnostic friend Professor Tyndall on a Sunday night. Though humanism has at some points diverged from Christian values, notably in the ethic of sex, its maturer forms still look remarkably like a de-dogmatized shell of Christianity, despite the protests of humanists to the contrary. Moreover, when humanists try, as they often do now, to give their creed more profundity, more inwardness, the closer it seems to be to what Christians have always believed.

The ideals of humanism are noble, but I question

whether they can be achieved by humanist means. 'Love your neighbour' is inadequate by itself. In the long run, to love God seems to be necessary, not only as the supreme end of man, but even as the means to enable him to love his neighbour. To achieve his aims the humanist may have to become a Christian.

But if Christianity is a fulfilment of humanism, it is also, I suggest, a fulfilment of existentialism. The existential categories are not far from those of Christianity. The sequence: dread, despair, the choice, commitment, authentic living, is closely parallel to Christian conversion: spiritual concern, sense of sin, trust in Christ, commitment, the recreated life. However the two sequences are not the same, and modern theology does Christianity an injustice when it makes them so. The first sequence is a shadow, a copy, of the second. The Christian version is the original.

The existential categories are the Christian categories emptied of their content and therefore, while deeply significant still, they lack direction or rationality. A leap – into nothing; commitment – only to a personal idea. This cannot lead to authentic living. But when these same categories are directed God-wards they make perfect sense. The free and authentic existence is the life whose meaning is love and whose purpose is the service of God.

So, illuminating though some of the insights of humanism and existentialism undoubtedly are, I believe that both are unrealistic. Neither gives an adequate philosophy of life. Neither is fully human. But the third, Christianity, cannot ultimately be judged by a mere comparison with other creeds. Its tenets are so absolute that it can only in the last resort be judged as true or false. The statement that in Jesus God was revealing himself to man; that in the death of Jesus God was reconciling man to himself; that in the resurrection of Jesus God was declaring the conquest of death for ever;

such claims cannot be reckoned as better or worse than another creed. They can only be judged as true or false.

But if they are true, there is no need to look beyond Christianity for the human way of life. If they are true. That is a question on which each must come to his own conviction.

# SELECTED BIBLIOGRAPHY

## Humanism

*H. J. Blackham, *Humanism* (Penguin Books).

J. S. Huxley (ed.), *The Humanist Frame* (Allen and Unwin).

*The Humanist Magazine* and other literature from the British Humanist Association.

J. Hemming, *Individual Morality* (Nelson).

A. E. E. McKenzie, *The Major Achievements of Science* (Cambridge University Press).

J. S. Mill, *On Liberty* (many editions).

A. O. J. Cockshutt, *The Unbelievers* (Collins).

*B. A. W. Russell, *Why I am not a Christian and Other Essays* (Allen and Unwin).

D. Morris, *The Naked Ape* (Corgi Books).

J. S. Huxley, *Evolutionary Ethics* (Pilot Press).

## Existentialism

*P. Roubiczek, *Existentialism, For and Against* (Cambridge University Press).

E. Mounier (trans. Eric Blow), *Existentialist Philosophies, an Introduction* (Barrie and Rockliff).

H. J. Blackham, *Six Existentialist Thinkers* (Routledge and Kegan Paul).

H. Hawton, *The Feast of Unreason* (Rationalist Press).

S. A. Kierkegaard, *Fear and Trembling* (Doubleday).

*F. Nietzsche, *Thus Spoke Zarathustra* (Penguin Books).

J.-P. Sartre, *The Diary of Roquentin* (Penguin Books).

F. Kafka, *The Trial* (Penguin Books).

A. Camus, *The Plague* (Penguin Books).

P. Tillich, *The Courage to Be* (Fontana Books).

## Christianity

*S. C. Neill, *A Genuinely Human Existence* (Constable).

A. Richardson, *Christian Apologetics* (SCM Press).

*P. Tournier, *The Meaning of Persons* (SCM Press).

M. Quoist, *The Christian Response* (Gill).

J. Baillie, *Invitation to Pilgrimage* (Penguin Books).

J. B. Phillips, *Ring of Truth* (Hodder and Stoughton).

J. Davidman, *Smoke on the Mountain* (Hodder and Stoughton).

C. S. Lewis, *Surprised by Joy* (Fontana Books).

W. N. Pittenger, *The Christian Understanding of Human Nature* (Nisbet).

E. M. B. Green, *Runaway World* (Inter-Varsity Press).

Two of the most important books in each section are marked with an asterisk.

# INDEX

Abyss, 74, 78, 79, 81–82, 90, 122, 127

Agnosticism, 10, 25–27, 30, 118, 135

Alienation, 55, 76, 106–111, 133

Aquinas, T., 15, 18, 128

Astronomy, 11, 16–18, 74

Atheism, 21, 36–39

Augustine, 15, 61, 64, 128

Authentic existence, 83–85, 117, 136

Authority, religious, 16–19, 25–26, 93, 127–129

Ayer, A. J., 28, 37

Barth, K., 63–64

Bentham, J., 21

Blackham, H. J., 38, 40, 50

Bonhoeffer, D., 39

Bradlaugh, C., 23, 37

British Humanist Association, 27, 28–33, 37, 49

Buber, M., 64–65, 80

Calvin, J., 128

Camus, A., 77–78

Commitment, 61–62, 83–85, 87, 91, 103, 127, 136

Comte, A., 22, 38

Conversion (*also* new birth), 39, 64, 111–117, 130, 132, 136

Creation, 95–99, 121

Criticism, biblical, 25, 63

Cross, the, 103, 110, 122–123, 136

Darwin, C. R., 23–26, 42–43, 55

Death, 37, 109, 115–116, 119, 130, 133

Democracy, 11, 21–22, 47

Developing countries, 8, 31–32

Eternal life, 102, 104, 115–116, 133–134

Ethics, 27, 34, 40–46, 52, 88, 104–106, 113, 125, 130, 132

Evidence for Christianity, 99, 109, 114, 121, 124–127

Evolution, 23–26, 40–46, 55, 95

Faith, 10, 30–31, 38–39, 45, 49–51, 62, 83, 121, 127–129

Forgiveness, 110–111, 113, 115, 117, 130, 132

Freedom, 81–84, 91, 96–97

Freud, S., 41, 72

Grace, 64, 111, 132

Greeks, 10–14, 47, 61

Guilt, 77, 90, 106–111, 130

Heidegger, M., 63, 65, 83
Huxley, J. S., 28, 38, 43–46, 131, 132
Huxley, T. H., 24, 42, 135

Jesus, 25, 99–100, 102–107, 110–112, 119, 120, 122–123, 126–127, 129, 132, 136
Job, 120–122

Kafka, F., 76–77, 110
Kierkegaard, S. A., 56–59, 62–63, 84, 128

Liberalism, Christian, 25–26, 39, 63–64, 112
Love, 31, 45, 48, 50, 58–59, 88–90, 92, 95–98, 101, 105, 106, 117, 123, 131

Meaninglessness (*also* absurdity), 62, 74–78, 90–91, 97–100, 118, 122, 128, 131
Mill, J. S., 21–22, 50
Mounier, E., 61–64

Nietzsche, F., 9, 56–61, 63, 65–74, 77–82, 87–91, 97, 102, 109
Pascal, B., 61–62
Paul, 64, 108, 113, 115
Pericles, 12
*Philosophes*, 20–21
Progress, belief in, 7, 22, 43–45, 50–51, 55, 68, 85–86, 130–133, 134
Psychology, 41, 59, 81, 125

Reason, 10–11, 18, 20–23, 31,

47, 52, 57–60, 64, 87, 124–127, 129
Religion, secular, 22, 26–27, 36–37, 49, 131
Responsibility, 30–31, 38, 40, 52, 81–85, 89, 91, 96–98, 108–111
Resurrection, 116, 126, 136
Russell, B. A. W., 28, 50, 93

Sartre, J.-P., 54, 63, 65, 72, 75–76, 84–85, 91, 106
Scientific method, 11, 16–18, 23–25, 46–47, 57–58, 85–86, 95, 125
Service, of mankind, 12–13, 31–33, 98, 104–106, 117, 123
Shaw, G. B., 27, 36
Sin (*also* moral failure), 50–52, 54–55, 70, 80, 85–86, 106–111, 113, 119, 130, 136
Spencer, H., 25, 40
Stephen, L., 40, 60
Suffering, 37, 78, 117–123, 130
Superman, overcoming man, 79–82, 111–117
Suicide, 7, 55, 75, 85, 91, 120

Theatre, modern, 54, 131
Tillich, P., 39, 111

Values, 52, 69, 73, 134, 135
Victorians, 21–27, 42, 52, 54–55, 70, 135
Voltaire, 20, 50–51

World peace, 32, 46, 47, 132, 134–135
Worship, 102, 134